"This book is so perfect that I only
got to hand deliver this book to Lar
taking such a beating since the su
son. It is perfect for them right now."

> —Charlie Walton, author of *When There Are No Words* and
> *Packing for the Big Trip*

"*Healing Together* is a beautiful book. It is clear, easy to read, and full of prag-
matic insights for couples facing the echoes of trauma. The authors tenderly
take a couple through issues such as dealing with anger and mourning loss and
offer strategies for healing and relationship renewal. This book is an invaluable
resource that will help couples face their traumas together."

> —Sue Johnson, Ph.D., professor of psychology at University
> of Ottawa and author of *Hold Me Tight*

"*Healing Together* is an essential resource for couples whose lives and relationships have been affected by traumatic experiences, and is particularly valuable for couples involved in police work, firefighting, emergency medical services, the military, and other professions where there is significant potential for
psychological trauma. Writing in a straightforward and down-to-earth style
that reflects the depth and breadth of the authors' experience working with
couples—including more than 400 couples involved in rescue and recovery in
the aftermath of 9/11—Suzanne Phillips and Dianne Kane provide a wealth
of information and insight into the nature of psychological trauma and its
emotional and behavioral consequences. As importantly, they provide effective
strategies and realistic solutions couples can use to restore and strengthen their
relationships. This is by far the best guide I've seen for couples affected by
trauma and post-traumatic stress."

> —Vincent E. Henry, CPP, Ph.D., associate professor and
> director of the Homeland Security Management Institute
> at Long Island University, and author of *Death Work*

"*Healing Together* is a gift to couples and a valuable resource for those who work with them. It sensitively illuminates the impact of trauma and PTSD on relationships in a way that empowers couples to understand, listen, mourn, cherish life's moments, and hope again. And Phillips' and Kane's contribution goes beyond the recovery of couples—it is a step both toward reducing the conspiracy of silence about the effects of trauma in families and toward preventing its intergenerational legacies."

—Yael Danieli, Ph.D., director of the Group Project for Holocaust Survivors and Their Children, past president and senior representative to the United Nations of the International Society for Traumatic Stress Studies

"*Healing Together* is profound in its scope and provides practical insights and skills that can be of enormous value to individuals and couples seeking a lasting change rather than a 'quick fix.' They will embark on an incredible journey with this book and ultimately be in control of their lives and their future. Phillips and Kane are to be applauded for their monumental work in the field of trauma and post-traumatic stress."

—Vali Stone, English professor at Georgian College and author of *Cops Don't Cry*

"Finally, a book providing psychological first aid for couples experiencing trauma and its devastating ripple effect on their relationship. Here, in clear language, men and women can learn for themselves about PTSD, destructive anger, triggers, memories, dreams, and sexual issues—what to do about them and how to know when professional help is needed. Indeed, a caring and compassionate mate aids recovery, but there are times when more is needed. Phillips and Kane provide sound information and exercises for 'healing together,' making this book a must-read for military and veteran couples and any couples or partners who have experienced the pain of trauma, loss, or disaster—all too many of us."

—Pauline Boss, author of *Loss, Trauma and Resilience* and *Ambiguous Loss*

"*Healing Together* is not only a guide for couples struggling to cope with trauma, but also a beacon of hope. Phillips and Kane do what no others have in one simple-to-read book—they show couples how working together as a team will speed recovery and protect their lifetime commitment."

—Charles R. Figley, Ph.D., author of *Helping Traumatized Families*

Healing Together

A Couple's Guide to Coping with Trauma & Post-Traumatic Stress

SUZANNE B. PHILLIPS, PSY.D., ABPP
DIANNE KANE, DSW

New Harbinger Publications, Inc.

Publisher's Note

This publication is designed to provide accurate and authoritative information in regard to the subject matter covered. It is sold with the understanding that the publisher is not engaged in rendering psychological, financial, legal, or other professional services. If expert assistance or counseling is needed, the services of a competent professional should be sought.

Distributed in Canada by Raincoast Books

Acquired by Melissa Kirk; Cover design by Amy Shoup;
Edited by Karen O'Donnell Stein; Text design by Tracy Carlson

Library of Congress Cataloging-in-Publication Data

Phillips, Suzanne B.
  Healing together : a couple's guide to coping with trauma and post-traumatic stress / Suzanne B. Phillips and Dianne Kane.
     p. cm.
  Includes bibliographical references.
  ISBN-13: 978-1-57224-544-0 (pbk. : alk. paper)
  ISBN-10: 1-57224-544-1 (pbk. : alk. paper) 1. Post-traumatic stress disorder--Patients--Family relationships.
2.   Psychic trauma--Patients--Family relationships. 3. Marital psychotherapy. I. Kane, Dianne. II. Title.
  RC552.P67P55 2008
  616.89'1562--dc22
                                     2008039788

14 13 12

10 9 8 7 6 5 4

For Kevin John Phillips, my husband of thirty-six years, my inspiration for loving, healing, and growing together.

—Suzanne Phillips

For Gordon Hawkins, who has surrounded me with beauty for over twenty years, and for Ian Hawkins, who has taught me so much about relationships.

—Dianne Kane

Contents

Acknowledgments

We would like to acknowledge those professional organizations, especially the New York City Fire Department–Counseling Service Unit and the American Group Psychotherapy Association, who have recognized and provided opportunities for our trauma work. We are very appreciative of the colleagues, family, and friends who recognized the need for this book and have been enthusiastically supportive of our efforts to make it happen. We are most grateful to the many couples who have faced trauma, trusted us with their pain, and impressed us with their resiliency and hope.

Introduction

You may have suffered the sudden and tragic loss of your child, witnessed the devastation of your home in a natural disaster, reeled from the impact of military deployment, struggled to conceive a child, or faced serious illness. Trauma, whether it happens to one or both partners, affects relationships. It disconnects you from your partner and often leaves you wondering how to find your way back to the safety of the relationship you once shared.

This book is a couple's guide for recovering from trauma. It is based on the recognition that, although couples naturally try to support each other, trauma can greatly strain and often disrupt the bond between them. Traumatic events are unexpected and often unimaginable. They always envolve loss. They assault your sense of self, your beliefs, and your view of the world as you knew it. Trauma robs you of a sense of safety because it suddenly alters what is familiar, including your connection with your partner. When you or your partner is hurt, grieving, having nightmares, unable to relax, too numb to feel, too angry to speak, or too sad to hope, both partners struggle and suffer. What you thought you knew about each other seems shaken, maybe lost. Blaming yourself or your partner, you may be unable to find the connection, the "we" that made you a couple.

The Goal of This Book

This book can help you recover and reconnect. It is based on the belief that, when trauma hits, a couple's relationship can be both the locus of pain and the source of support and recovery. Accordingly, this book is not simply a guide to a happier relationship. Nor is it just a book about trauma. It is a guide for recovery after you or your partner has suffered some type of trauma and is feeling its impact on your relationship.

This book will tell you what the experts know about the impact of and recovery from trauma in a way that is specifically relevant to and usable by couples. It will help you and your partner make sense of what you are experiencing in a way that reduces anxiety and makes you feel less helpless. Understanding what has happened will make you both feel that you have more control over your lives and your future. You will be guided as you adopt new coping skills and identify and use the strength and resiliency you have both always drawn upon.

A Word About Us

In our work with couples for over twenty-five years and with more than three hundred couples who worked in rescue and recovery in the aftermath of 9/11, we have found that in the months and even years after trauma, couples often feel helpless, angry, bereft, and isolated from each other. Many are embarrassed that they are having trouble and are reluctant to talk about it or seek help. Many privately fear that, in addition to all they have lost, they might also lose their relationship. This book is based upon our observation that demystifying trauma and recovery for couples and offering strategies to enhance the safety, trust, and intimacy of their bond are powerful tools for recovery.

How to Use This Book

The book is divided into six chapters. Chapter 1 offers an understanding of trauma and how it looks by inviting you to consider trauma through the eyes of different couples. Chapter 2 defines and teaches a couple's version of psychological first aid, a natural and informal system that partners can use to help lower the impact of trauma on one another.

In chapter 3, we will discuss the relationship between anger and trauma and the ways in which anger masks feelings like helplessness, shame, and loss. We'll look at issues such as "the fight worth having," behaviors that serve to fuel the fight, anger management for couples, and the role of forgiveness. Chapter 4 offers ways to recapture and reclaim your intimacy and sexual connection. We'll address the impact of sexual and nonsexual trauma on sexual desire and functioning and offer strategies for dealing with the fallout from post-traumatic stress symptoms. We'll clarify the concepts of desire and receptivity, the meaning of saying yes and saying no, capturing and keeping the romantic moment, and dealing with pornography. Chapter 5 helps you find a place for the trauma. It guides you toward understanding and helps you work together to integrate traumatic memories, utilize dreams, and rescript nightmares. Chapter 6 invites you to recognize and enhance your resilience as a couple as you move into your future. We'll discover how to use that resilience for healing in connection with your personal attributes, hardiness, positive outlook, problem-solving skills, laughter, and shared values. You'll consider the meaning of hope and the possibility of post-traumatic growth. In total, the chapters offer you understanding and skills to bring you together through this journey that you never expected to take.

Why This Book Can Help

You are not alone in the experience of trauma. Reading this book, considering the examples, and trying out the strategies will allow you to understand this. It will help you see that much of what you have been experiencing is normal in the context of the trauma you have been through and assist you in finding a way to recover and move on. Here are some of the benefits you will experience from working through this book:

- You will come to understand that trauma to one or both partners affects a couple in a way that is more than the sum of the individual responses.

- You will find that having information about trauma lowers anxiety and feelings of helplessness.

- You may see yourselves in the examples of other couples, and this will help you understand what is happening in your relationship.

* You will find that understanding fosters empathy for yourself and your partner and reduces isolation and despair.

* You may feel less worried and better able to utilize your strengths and develop additional coping skills.

* Your increased understanding of trauma and the road to recovery will help you make decisions, if needed, about seeking professional help.

* You may see that there can be a way to deal with loss and redefine your life together.

* You may find that your relationship is a crucial resource in the face of trauma and a significant factor in your recovery.

* You will see that marriages and relationships need not be the collateral damage of traumatic life events.

Making this Book Work for You

This book may be used to offer understanding and hope in different ways. It can be read by both of you as a couple or by either partner. Whether or not you have both directly faced the trauma, you have each experienced its impact on your relationship and can thus benefit from this expanded understanding of trauma and the path toward recovery.

Although reading this book as a couple might be a wonderful goal, you do not need to wait until that is possible. It can be helpful for both of you if only one partner reads the book. Sometimes one partner might talk about something he or she has read or even read a section to the other that has particular relevance, and this may help the other partner to consider the issue. Sometimes nothing overt is said, but the partner who has read the book might bring greater understanding and empathy to the relationship; this inevitably changes the atmosphere, the tone, the touch, and your pattern of relating. Partners have both conscious and unconscious awareness of each other. It is precisely for this reason that they share the impact of trauma and can utilize their bond for recovery.

As you'll discover, each of the chapters in this book offers information and strategies that address those aspects of relationships most affected by trauma. We recommend that you and your partner consider utilizing these as part of your recovery process. The strategies and guidelines cover a broad range of topics and include creating a safe couple space, stress reduction, being a compassionate presence, communicating needs, listening skills, defusing anger, fair fighting, recovering from sexual trauma, renewing your sexual relationship, dream collaboration, use and misuse of outside social support, reflecting on post-traumatic growth, and others. Each strategy has been designed to offer you and your partner coping skills and nonthreatening opportunities to move you through your journey to recovery.

Understanding the nature of trauma and recovery has made a difference in our own lives and in the lives of those couples we have had the privilege to work with. We believe that gaining this understanding will make a difference in your relationship too. We invite you to go forward, believing in the power of healing.

1

Something Traumatic Has Happened

Since we cannot change reality, let us change
the eyes which see reality.

—Nikos Kazantzakis (2003)

If you are reading this book, then something traumatic has happened in your life. It may have been the two minutes you could never prepare for—the accident, the hurricane, the sudden death of a loved one, an unexpected military deployment, or a childbirth that has taken an extraordinary physical and emotional toll. This chapter begins your journey toward recovery. It is based on the recognition that trauma will affect both partners in a relationship, and that any traumatic experience will also affect the relationship you share. We are talking about more than secondary traumatic stress (the theory that close connection with a traumatized person can cause a partner to experience the same symptoms as the traumatized partner; Arzi, Solomon, and Dekel 2000; Figley 1983). In this book, we are talking about the fact that partners may react to trauma in similar or different ways, but—by virtue of their conscious and unconscious connection—the relationship they share, the "we" they experience, will inevitably change. The nature of this change is complex but it need not be destructive. Above and beyond the particular situation you and your partner are facing, know that your relationship gives both of you the most important resource for trauma recovery: human connection. In this chapter we offer you the first step in using the potential of your relationship. We will clarify what trauma is and its impact on relationships in a way that helps you understand and deal with your own reactions, the reactions of your partner, and the dynamics that unfold between you.

What Is Trauma?

In medical terms, a trauma is defined as a serious injury or shock to the body that might result from violence or an accident. From a psychological perspective it is defined as an event that has the capacity to provoke fear, helplessness, or horror in response to the threat of injury or death (American Psychiatric Association 2000). In broader terms, a traumatic event is one of extreme stress that outstrips a person's ability to cope. In most cases it is an unimaginable event and out of the range of what you expected to handle. You were not supposed to be wounded in combat, lose a baby, watch your home be destroyed by fire, or be diagnosed with serious illness. Trauma affects you emotionally, cognitively, and physically. It violates your belief in yourself, your judgment, your body, other people, even higher powers.

Trauma Involves Loss

Trauma always involves loss. Whether a traumatic event has threatened your life, robbed you of someone you love, or destroyed your community, it deprives you—suddenly and even violently—of what you had. It destroys the sense of safety, predictability, and justice that you assumed and expected in your life. The reality of such a loss is often overshadowed by the physical and psychological impact of the trauma or the circumstances of the trauma itself. This in turn can interfere with feeling entitled to or being able to grieve. Sometimes the loss is so overwhelmingly clear that for a time it is too much to face. Sometimes a loss is ambiguous, as in an unclear medical prognosis or the unexplained absence of a loved one. In any case, sadness and grief are human and inevitable in the experience of trauma.

Trauma Affects Relationships

When people fall in love and marry or enter into a committed relationship, the relationship gives new meaning to definitions of self, other, and the rest of the world. As part of a "we," each person in a healthy relationship feels connected, valued, loved, and desired. As a result of the relationship each feels safe, empowered, and happy. Something wonderful has happened! Notwithstanding the ebb and flow of time, the way they fight, the passion they show, the bills they pay, the number of children they have, or the number of years that pass in stress or bliss, most young and old couples develop a defined and familiar experience of each other. They share a conscious and unconscious bond. They play certain roles in each other's lives. She makes him laugh, he confides in her, she worries too much, he silently supports, she reminds him of his talents, he makes her feel desired, he owns the remote, and she buys the furniture.

Trauma disrupts the patterns of attachment and care that a couple has developed. Trauma puts up a wall that for a time locks a couple out of their familiar world and leaves them frozen in the traumatic event. Suddenly there is no past, and the future feels impossible. What they believed before and their dreams about the future no longer feel relevant, much less possible.

How Does Trauma Play Out in a Relationship?

Following are a few examples of how trauma can disrupt the familiar world of a healthy relationship:

After her boyfriend, a policeman, was hurt in the line of duty, Mary couldn't just go to sleep and expect that he would be safe. Every night the worry crept in.

After breast cancer, Sue stopped believing she could ever be desirable again and avoided her husband, Carl.

After his brother was killed in Iraq, Mike pulled back on the sense of humor that had been so basic to the shared connection between him and his fiancée, Jill.

Patty and Sean began to doubt that they could rebuild their house, much less their life, after the hurricane—how can you feel capable of anything if you can't prevent bad things from happening?

One expert suggests that a person who has been traumatized has been "wounded by reality." There is a disruption in the core self, "quite literally fixing it in place, changing biology and psychic experience" (Boulanger 2002, 45, 54). This translates to a loss of the familiar sense of self, belief in one's abilities, and trust in one's judgment. It makes sense that, if you are suddenly uncertain regarding what has happened and who you are, you will be uncertain of your partner and how he or she will respond to you. Other experts (McFarlane and Girolamo 1996) suggest that traumatic events violate our existing ways of making sense of our reactions, change our perceptions of other people's behavior, and alter the framework we use for interacting with the world. Accordingly, when your view of the world and your perception of others change, your familiar expectations and patterns as a couple are shaken. For a time you may both feel lost. Working together, however, you can regain your bond and the patterns between you may actually become stronger.

The Usual Responses to Trauma

Most people respond to catastrophic and traumatic events with distress. It is a normal reaction to the horror, helplessness, and fear that make up the crucial components of a traumatic experience (McFarlane and Yehuda 1996). The symptoms of distress reflect the fact that trauma jolts the mind and body—we are wired to respond to trauma physically, neurochemically, and emotionally. The distress symptoms, which will be defined next, include *intrusion or reexperiencing*; *hyperarousal*; and *constriction, numbing, and avoidance* (Herman 1997). Often appearing within the first days after a trauma, these symptoms, although intense at first, generally subside with time for many survivors. As will be discussed at a later point, if these symptoms become a persistent pattern lasting more than one month they are described as *post-traumatic stress disorder* (PTSD). However, even when the disorder does not occur, one or more of these symptoms can cause distress to an individual and his or her partner. Understanding these symptoms of trauma can be a first step in managing their impact on your relationship.

Intrusion or Reexperiencing

Intrusion or reexperiencing is like being caught in an indelible imprint of the traumatic moment. In some cases intrusive symptoms may appear within the first forty-eight hours after trauma (Shalev 1992). It is as if the hospital scene, the oncoming car, or the explosion were being played over and over again. Such symptoms translate into nightmares, flashbacks, fear of going to sleep, and traumatic memories. Although such intrusive symptoms are frightening and bewildering, it is worth underscoring that they are actually functional. They are the mind and body's way of *assimilating* or fitting a physically and emotionally incomprehensible event into one's existing life experience. For some, the intrusion brings with it self-recriminations about what else they could or should have done. As we will discuss later on in this book, sharing these nightmares or flashbacks actually helps you to get clarity on the event, lessens the intensity of the memory, and gives you a way to integrate what has happened into the framework of your life.

Hyperarousal

Hyperarousal is the persistent expectation of being in danger. In everyday life, hyperarousal translates into an inability to relax; an exaggerated startle response; difficulties with sleep; irritability; quick triggers to anger; and hypersensitivity to noise, smells, tastes, and so on. It is as if the body remains ready for fight or flight. The person has no sense of finally being safe even though the accident is past, Iraq is behind him, or the cancer is in remission. Once the actual traumatic event is over, the acute arousal is driven by the continual reexperiencing, reappraisal, and triggering of the traumatic memories. Although this hyperarousal is a normal neurophysiological response to a traumatic event, it is often so disruptive that a person will develop destructive coping mechanisms, like drinking excessively, to calm down and get some sleep.

Sometimes, as in the case of police or military personnel, a certain level of hyperarousal is integral to the person's ability to fulfill the job or to complete the mission. However, when this functional level of hyperarousal is outstripped by the symptoms described previously, then it's clear that this is a traumatic response. As we will discuss further on, understanding this phenomenon helps both partners recognize the reactions and permits them to consider safe and constructive ways to respond.

Constriction, Numbing, and Avoidance

Constriction and numbing are responses to trauma that involve a form of physical and psychological shutdown. It is normal to freeze in the face of danger or traumatic and unthinkable loss. (Levine 1997). Think, for example, of some animals, such as the possum, which plays dead to fool its predator. As is the case with the other responses to trauma, the persistence of this appropriate fight-or-flight response can interfere with functioning and recovery. When numbing persists it often translates into avoidance, isolation, withdrawal, or fatigue. Though intrusive symptoms often remain the same or decrease with time, avoidance of reminders of the event will frequently increase in those people who have developed PTSD (Shalev 1992). Sometimes people are so upset by their own stress reactions that they begin to organize their lives so they can avoid anything that might trigger memories or feelings related to the trauma. Sometimes the avoidance takes the form of drug or alcohol use.

In a couple, such avoidance and withdrawal is often interpreted by the other partner as rejection and loss of interest in the relationship. This is a common misperception. It often helps both partners to consider that one partner's avoidance of and withdrawal from people and social events may actually be an attempt to regulate panic, anxiety, or triggers of traumatic feelings and memories—all common symptoms in the aftermath of traumatic events. When you understand the cause, you can work together to regulate activities in a way that better accommodates both of your needs.

Post-traumatic Stress Disorder (PTSD)

A person is diagnosed with PTSD after exposure to a traumatic event that involves actual or threatened death or serious injury to self or others, and for which the person has responded with fear, helplessness, or horror. PTSD also includes the persistence of the three distinct types of symptoms—intrusion (reexperiencing), numbing (avoidance), and hyperarousal—for a least one month after the traumatic event (American Psychiatric Association 2000). It is important to understand that experiencing such stress symptoms immediately after a traumatic event does not automatically indicate post-traumatic stress disorder.

Even for the most acute traumas most of the symptoms of intrusion, numbing, and hyperarousal will be resolved within the first month, although some symptoms might persist for a longer time in a less intense way. For a minority of people, a persistent pattern of symptoms will endure beyond one month and will result in PTSD. A partner's early understanding of these symptoms and support for handling them becomes a very important factor in the suffering partner's acceptance, assimilation, and recovery.

Factors Affecting a Person's Response to Trauma

How you or your partner responds to trauma will have to do with the nature of the traumatic event, how much you both were directly exposed to or affected by the event, and the meaning of the event to each of you. In addition, response is affected by your own history, personal characteristics, and resiliency traits, as well as the response of other people, be it concern or blame.

Characteristics of the Traumatic Event

Judith Herman, a renowned trauma theorist, tells us, "At the moment of trauma, the victim is rendered helpless by overwhelming force. When that force is that of nature, we speak of disasters. When the force is that of other human beings, we speak of atrocities" (Herman 1997, 33).

As a result, traumatic events such as rape, assault, or terrorist attack may engender more fear, rage, blame, and helplessness than trauma from natural causes. Working through such trauma may be more complex than recovery from natural disasters. Some events are so horrific that nearly everyone exposed to them will have a strong reaction. Terrorist attacks like 9/11 or natural disasters like Hurricane Katrina, which cause extensive loss of life and personal property, are likely to create significant distress. Still, the intensity and length of people's responses will be different for each individual.

Intensity of and Proximity to the Event

The severity of a traumatic event and a person's proximity and exposure to the event are likely to affect the nature of their response. Direct exposure to events that threaten one's life or someone else's life will create distress in most people and will likely be manifested in symptoms such as intrusion, hyperarousal, and numbing or constriction. The greater the intensity and loss connected with the event, as well as the length of time that the person had to endure the event, the greater the impact it is likely to have on a given individual. Thus, the person trapped for a long time in a car after a serious accident is likely to be at greater risk for symptoms compared with someone who is quickly rescued. The farther away a person is from the actual trauma (for example, a person who witnesses the accident from afar), the more likely it is that this person's response will reflect his or her own personal life experience and not simply the traumatic event itself. Consider this example:

> Both Mark and Karen were at the stadium when the man a few seats down suffered a heart attack and died. Given that Karen's father had also died from a heart attack, she was far more upset and traumatized by the event than Mark was.

Characteristics of the Person Experiencing the Event

Trauma is very much determined by who a person is. Childhood history, prior trauma, gender, and age will very much determine a person's reaction to an event. Those who have successfully handled other difficult, stressful situations may actually find it easier to cope with the trauma.

However, it is also possible that those who have faced other emotionally challenging situations, such as serious illness or early parental loss, may have a more intense traumatic reaction to an additional stressful event.

What is traumatic for one individual may be less so for another. This is important to understand, especially if you and your partner have experienced the same event but are reacting quite differently to it. This was true in the case of Lynn and Mike.

When she suffered a miscarriage in the beginning of her third month, Lynn was devastated. Then in her late thirties, she was worried that this might be their only chance to have a child. Often unable to concentrate or sleep, she would ruminate and blame herself for waiting until her career was set before starting a family. Lynn was further upset by Mike's reaction. He was upset by the loss but he seemed confident that there would be other chances. Lynn wondered why he wasn't blaming himself for their decision to wait to have kids. When she questioned him about this, he felt that she was blaming and judging him, and this often led to tension and fighting.

Resiliency Traits

Resiliency comes from traits that have enabled a person to succeed or cope with challenges or traumatic events. Generally these traits include intelligence, physical strength, athleticism, creativity, artistic ability, social skills, problem-solving ability, moral code, independence, spirituality, and interpersonal connections. As will be discussed in later chapters, in the aftermath of trauma, when everything seems impossible, partners often need to remind each other of their resilience. You can often begin to move forward when you remember who you are and the strengths that have helped you cope in the past. This proved helpful for Marilyn and Dave when they faced the loss of their son:

When soldiers appeared at their door to report that their son was killed in Iraq, Marilyn and Dave could barely breathe. They felt dazed and immobilized. It was Marilyn who somehow managed to ask her sister to call their minister, since she knew that in the past their spiritual strength had gotten them through.

Response of Others

A supportive social network, including peers (other people who have experienced a similar trauma), family members, spouse or significant other, and society in general, can be a significant factor in a person's recovery from trauma. As we saw happen with Vietnam veterans, when the culture translated disapproval of the war to the denigration of its warriors, recovery and healing become tragically compromised. The burden of other people's judgments can be seen in pain experienced by Lauren and Roy after their child was hurt:

> *The nanny frantically called Lauren and Roy when their daughter was injured in an accident at the playground. They raced to meet them at the hospital, where the doctors said that they could save Sara's eye but many surgeries would be necessary and recovery would be slow. Heartbroken, self-blaming, Lauren and Roy attempted to console each other with the reality that this type of accident can happen no matter who is caring for a three-year-old. The look on Lauren's mother's face, however, whenever she reminded them that they were both at work the day of the accident, spoke volumes and kept their pain and guilt going.*

Given that we cannot always change the way people react to us, a couple's ability to understand and support each other becomes even more important. Experts suggest that your ability to experience comfort from another human being in the aftermath of trauma is a more important determinant of recovery than the trauma itself (van der Kolk, Perry, and Herman 1991). The entire recovery process is helped by the presence of an informed, compassionate social network. As partners you are the most important people in that network.

Understanding the Impact of Trauma on Couples

It is important to remember that just because a couple experiences symptoms after a traumatic event does not mean that they did not have a good relationship, were not strong, or were never truly in love. It means that something occurred that was beyond what they could have physically or emotionally expected. The couples described in this section did not plan to suffer, withdraw, become irritable, feel numb, criticize each other, or feel despair. But because of the trauma they had experienced, they could not access their strengths. They could not find their similarities and they could not tolerate their differences. Let's look at how the particular symptoms of trauma can affect relationships.

The following example of Miguel and Jane shows how difficult it can be for partners to connect when one is experiencing symptoms of hyperarousal.

Returning from Afghanistan after two tours as a marine, Miguel was restless. It seemed as if he just could not sit still or relax. Jane had been counting the days waiting for his return. When he stepped off the plane Miguel seemed so excited to see her. During his first days home he seemed to want to spend time catching up with everything he had left behind, even the many neglected home maintenance items he used to hate.

Gradually, it began to seem as if Miguel needed to keep himself distracted. He just could not sit with Jane and watch a sitcom before going to bed, something they had enjoyed almost daily. Instead he spent hours surfing the Web. He seemed hyper and had to keep both his mind and body moving. Jane experienced this as rejection, wondering why he didn't want to spend time with her the way he had before. When Jane tried to bring it up or ask Miguel to shut off the computer and come to bed, he would act annoyed. Still, she was so happy to have him home that she did not want to risk upsetting him further. She tried telling herself she should be patient, and that maybe tomorrow would be different. Still she worried and wondered what was wrong.

Tony and Linda's struggle exemplifies how the symptoms of intrusion and reexperiencing can keep a couple unable to shake the impact of trauma.

Tony and Linda found each other later in life and fell in love quickly. They and their families were thrilled that after disappointments earlier in life these two people would have a chance to enjoy a full life together. They moved in together after a few months of dating, and their commitment to one another could not have been stronger. Then while they were on vacation, Tony had a sudden heart attack, and he had bypass surgery shortly after. Linda was sure he would not make it. Now, six months later, Tony was back at work and he was ready for them to go on with their lives and plan for the future. But Linda could not relax. She worried about his health, checked what he ate, and argued about how he was taking care of himself. Whenever she saw anything that looked like pain on his face she became anxious. Even the thought of a vacation brought back the panic of the heart attack. She just could not get the pictures out of her head.

Constriction and avoidance in Sally and Nate's relationship kept them at a distance from each other after losing their baby.

Sally and Nate's daughter was born prematurely, with heart and lung complications. They were very close and supportive of each other in those first weeks—together they were on a mission to keep her alive. They alternated shifts at the hospital and held each other at night when they cried and worried about the future.

Six months after her death, everyone was expecting them to be feeling better, even hinting about them having another baby. This was the worst time. They could barely find themselves, much less each other. By busying themselves with work and chores they were avoiding each other. It was as if togetherness was a reminder of their false hope, of their enormous loss. They had been vigilant while holding on to each other through the crisis, but now, on the other side of the loss, they could barely feel. Romance seemed irrelevant—maybe even inappropriate or irreverent. How could they go back to a happy life? It wasn't supposed to be this way!

Different Ways of Coping

Often a person's or couple's greatest source of distress comes not from the traumatic event itself but the persistence of symptoms of intrusion, hyperarousal, and avoidance over time (McFarlane and Yehuda 1996). It is important to consider that, just as you and your partner may define a traumatic event differently, it is possible that you may cope quite differently with trauma symptoms. We see this in the reactions of Marie and Chris.

Marie just could not stop telling the story of the hurricane that had destroyed their house and their belongings and almost killed her and Chris, her husband of six months. She would repeatedly go into detail about how they had to swim out the front door, how she got caught on debris and Chris had to go underwater to untangle her. The problem was that every time she described the trauma of that night, Chris felt thrown back into it—the panic, the fear that he would lose her, the near-drowning. To cope with the feelings, he would walk into another room or go outside. Not understanding the impact that she was having on him, Marie resented his pulling away whenever she retold the experience. She wondered why he wouldn't want to be close to her at those times. Not recognizing that Marie's repetitive descriptions were a desperate attempt to calm herself down, Chris felt isolated and ignored. Neither recognized the effect of their necessary but different coping styles.

The Road to Recovery

Trauma theorist Judith Herman (1997) tells us that recovery unfolds in three stages: (1) establishing safety, (2) remembering and mourning, and (3) reconnecting with ordinary life.

Though establishing safety is crucial for setting recovery into place, there is no rigid sequence to these stages. At different times and in different ways, people try to move from feelings of danger to safety, from intrusive images and nightmares to more tolerable memories, from acknowledging loss to reclaiming hope, and from feelings of isolation to reconnection. Let's take a closer look at these three stages.

Establishing Safety

Traumatic events often leave a person feeling that he or she is still in danger. You or your partner may have been in danger of dying or witnessed death. As a result, you may have experienced feelings of extreme helplessness, pain, or loss. In situations like this, people often feel unsafe in their bodies and confused in their thinking. They might even fear that they are going crazy.

Moving away from this state of fear and toward establishing safety starts with the body. Getting proper medical attention and taking care to reset your body rhythms—sleeping, eating, resting, and exercising—helps get you back to physical safety. Naming what happened as *trauma* and seeing your reactions as normal provide emotional safety. These are major steps toward feeling more in control, creating order out of chaos, and finding safety in the aftermath of danger.

> *Once John and Sue realized that it was not so unusual for a veteran, home from Iraq, to wake up startled in the middle of the night and feel compelled to check the perimeter of the house, they both were less worried and frightened.*

> *When Linda and Eric understood that after a rape a woman takes a while to feel safe with anyone, she felt less guilty about not wanting sex and he felt less rejected.*

It should be noted that "safety" may have different meanings for different people. Even partners who have directly shared the same trauma may need different things in order to feel safe. Some, for example, need to be surrounded by friends and family; others need privacy and a feeling that they can control what unfolds in their environment.

> *In the aftermath of 9/11, Rob, a firefighter, and his wife, Kristin, knew that when it came to extended family events, she preferred to go with the children and be surrounded with people, and Rob needed and valued the time alone to recharge by reading or going to the gym. Despite comments and criticism by neighbors and family, both partners understood the need for this arrangement, and it worked for them.*

The presence of a significant other, a partner who understands and accepts that there can be different ways of feeling safe, reduces the feeling of being crazy, frightened, or alone. Feeling safe in your primary relationship is a crucial place to begin to rebuild trust and safety in your world.

Remembering and Mourning

This stage involves transforming a traumatic memory into an integrated part of one's history. It means remembering in order to make meaning of what happened and to mourn what was lost. Traumatic memories are static, highly emotional, repetitive clips, dreams, and flashbacks of some aspect of the horror you have experienced. It is as if the story of your life has suddenly been disrupted by an event that doesn't fit—and the result is like a book with a page torn out, a jigsaw puzzle with a missing piece.

Within this stage there are three steps that move traumatic memories and the loss associated with them into a different way of remembering and experiencing.

Revisiting the Trauma

Both safety and courage are needed for revisiting the trauma. There is a fine line between revisiting and feeling retraumatized by memories of the traumatic experience. Each person needs to feel safe and be able to hold on to that safety when he or she chooses to revisit the trauma. The partners have to be able to slowly return to the memory of the trauma with less and less terror, guilt, blame, or shame. Time and certain circumstances may be needed before such safety is possible. Because all trauma involves loss, sometimes a person or couple has to be able or ready to mourn the loss caused by the trauma before they can revisit the trauma itself.

Bearing Witness

Once a person can return psychologically to the traumatic event, others—in many cases the person's partner—can play an important role in validating the experience. Bearing witness to your partner's feelings, thoughts, dreams, and memories, often by just listening, offers a powerful recognition of what has been suffered in a way that reduces emotional pain and feelings of isolation.

Reconstructing the Event

We know that the action of telling a story in a safe and protected relationship can actually produce changes in the way the brain processes a traumatic memory (Herman 1997, 183). At the time of the traumatic event, the right side of the brain, alerted for danger, registers the image, smell, taste, and touch of trauma in a way that is different from what happens in day-to-day narrative memories. Once the person is in a place of emotional safety, however, a person's opportunity to reconstruct the traumatic memory, to actually put words to it, provides the chance to reconfigure the experience with the verbal, linguistic left side of the brain (Schore 2003). Eventually the traumatic event becomes part of the person's life story and can be told without triggering the pain and emotions of the trauma. Instead of being haunted by it, a person can choose whether or not to think about it.

Mourning the Loss

Mourning the loss that follows in the aftermath of trauma happens in incremental steps. Such mourning is central to integrating trauma into the story of your life. People often fear that revisiting trauma will leave them crying forever or force them to give up the connection with their lost loved one. As a couple, you will see that remembering and mourning the trauma is about slowly facing and redefining loss. It is about supporting each other with new ways of remembering those who were lost and embracing their essence as you go forward. It is about connecting again.

After the accident, Tina could not talk about what had happened. Everyone told her that given the weather and the time of night there was no way she could have seen the child run into the street. Still, she blamed herself and refused to talk about it to anyone, even Alan, her fiancé. Unlike others, Alan did not push Tina to talk about it. He just stayed by her side and continued to plan for their future. At times she could not believe that he still wanted to be with her. Alan also encouraged her to spend time with his nieces and nephews, letting her know that he trusted them in her care. Again Tina was surprised. Then one day, seemingly out of the blue, Tina told Alan all about it. She described the night it happened and, equally important, all the terrible things she had been thinking and telling herself ever since. Alan just held her as she cried and told her story. After that night, Tina mentioned it more often and more easily. She would mention the things that pulled her back to that awful night—the rain, a certain type of twilight, a bad dream—and now she seemed less distraught when she was pulled back. When she was feeling emotionally stronger and safer, she told Alan how much she appreciated his silent support—how much that had meant to her at a time when everyone else had seemed full of advice.

Reconnection

If our earliest childhood attachments were positive, then we have the sense that we are not alone, that we are psychologically connected and safe. If we are in a good relationship, we carry the sense of someone else being there for us. One of the most devastating and pervasive effects of trauma is that it disconnects people from everything they trusted and isolates them with feelings of shame, blame, loss, and often despair. Even if a large number of people have suffered from the same natural disaster or both partners have faced the same trauma, individuals are often left feeling isolated and different from the rest of the world.

Reconnection is the final and most crucial stage of recovery from trauma and it may be the stage most affected by the presence of a partner. In the previous example, Alan's continued love and support of Tina, who had disconnected from her good self and lost the belief that anyone could forgive or trust her, was vital to her recovery and their future together. Like Tina, you are walking through this with another person whose love for you can help reinstate your sense of being good and lovable, and your ability to be hopeful and recover.

Starting the Healing Process

You may recognize yourself in some of the examples of other couples who have faced trauma. If so, it is likely that you are wondering what you and your partner can do. If you are reading this book you have already started doing something.

Throughout the book you will find suggested exercises and coping strategies that you can work on alone or together as a couple. We offer them as a way to begin to apply the ideas in the chapter to your specific situation. Some may feel right to you; others may seem forced. Trust your gut and do what feels helpful. Use the pages at the end of this book to make notes or use a separate notebook that you can keep for this purpose. If you are reading this book together you may want to combine your responses in one place, or you may each want a separate notebook to share when you are ready.

Exercise: Finding a Safe Couple Place

There are two important reasons for this first exercise. First, finding ways to feel physically and psychologically safe is crucial in trauma recovery. This exercise is one of many techniques you will learn to use when you or your partner needs to feel safe. Second, this exercise asks you to reach back behind the wall of trauma to your past. Trauma experts remind us that it is very important to reclaim what you had before the trauma in order to create continuity in your life and heal the rupture from the trauma. In this exercise we invite you to reclaim something that you had with your partner, specifically a safe and wonderful place. It belongs to you. It is still a part of your history.

1. Try to remember a place that you associate with being happy, peaceful, and content with your partner. It may be a certain vacation, an apartment, a city, a restaurant, even a car. Once you have identified the place, just thinking "Bermuda," "the green Mustang," or "our place on Smith Street" can bring you back to that feeling of safety.

2. Write this place down in the space provided or in your notebook. Label it as your safe place together. This place is your place, and it is a valuable resource in your recovery process.

3. When you are ready, ask your partner if there is a place that he or she always associates with your being together in a happy and contented way. Ask your partner to also write that place down. You need not identify the same place as your partner.

4. If it feels comfortable, share your safe place with your partner. Did you both choose the same place? Are you surprised that they are the same? Or that your partner has thought of another safe place? Write down the names of these locations and identify them as your "couple safe places."

Summary

The goal of this first chapter has been to begin to restore some control and connection in your life together by making sense of what you have been through. Toward this end, we have discussed the meaning and impact of trauma in relation to common reactions; couple responses; the need for establishing safety; and remembering, mourning, and reconnecting as important steps toward recovery.

As the following chapters guide you to understand and deal with the traumatic events that you have faced, hold on to your "couple safe places" and carry them in your minds and hearts. When you are feeling anxious or scared or lost in the relationship, you may find it helpful to think of your safe place and derive strength and hope from revisiting it.

Don't worry if your partner cannot or will not participate. Don't create pressure on yourself or your partner to share your safe space. Partners recover at different paces. You will both benefit even if for now only one of you can find the safe place you once shared.

2

Couples Psychological First Aid

Pain shared is pain divided.

—Lt. Col. Dave Grossman (2004)

In the immediate aftermath of trauma and disaster, many people are left feeling numb, confused, and disoriented. They can't believe what has happened. They may reexperience the event in flashbacks; they may be unable to calm down or sleep. Some may want to talk about what has happened. Many may be unable to find words. Some may want to avoid anything related to the event. These are all normal reactions that usually subside within a month, although flare-ups can occur for quite a while. Most people will not need professional help, but almost all will benefit from support. One of the most recommended ways of providing that support in the first hours and weeks after a traumatic event is to administer psychological first aid.

Medical first aid is basic emergency care that is given immediately to a wounded person for the purpose of minimizing injury and future disability. It can be provided by a trained layperson. In a similar way, psychological first aid involves providing human connection, safety, basic needs, information, and support for the purpose of reducing initial distress and preventing long-term emotional suffering.

We have observed that, despite pain, blame, or separation, partners often have a more soothing physical and emotional impact on each other than anyone else. They want a way to be there for each other, and psychological first aid seems both a natural and effective response for partners. Just as most families keep some first aid supplies on hand for emergencies, most couples have some supplies of compassion, support, and empathy in their relationship to draw upon when facing traumatic events.

The goal of this chapter is to define and demonstrate couples psychological first aid. In describing psychological first aid, the Institute of Medicine (IOM) states that it "provides individuals with skills they can use in responding to psychological consequences of (disasters) in their own lives, as well as in the lives of their family, friends, and neighbors" (IOM 2003, 4–7). In other words, it is psychological first aid *by the couple* and *for the couple*.

Too often, in the aftermath of trauma, one partner steps up to be there for the other, or both unrelentingly take on the crisis, but the relationship falters under the unexpected pressure. Couples psychological first aid tries to account for the "me, you, and we" in a relationship. It recognizes that couples often have a great deal to offer each other but are uncertain how to proceed. It offers four principles to guide you in responding to each other as well as in safeguarding and supporting the relationship you share.

Four Principles of Couples Psychological First Aid

1. Be a compassionate presence for each other

2. Establish physical and psychological safety

3. Identify and respond to needs

4. Offer practical assistance and support coping skills

Some of these principles may validate what you are already doing. Some may appear simplistic or too subtle to be of much value in the face of what feels like such a large disturbance in your relationship. As you come to understand the rationale for their use, you may see that each in its own way can make a significant contribution to the process of recovery. Many of these actions can be applied in different ways, depending on who you are, what feels most natural to you, and what has been typical of your relationship.

Principle 1: Being a Compassionate Presence for Each Other

Compassion is defined as "deep awareness of the suffering of another coupled with the wish to relieve it" (American Heritage Dictionary 1993, 284). Consciously trying to be a compassionate presence may be the most valuable assistance you can offer one another. We believe that being a compassionate presence to your partner is based on two important concepts—the power of attachment and the gift of containment.

The Power of Attachment

The physical presence of another who is compassionate and concerned can help reduce hyperarousal and stress in the aftermath of trauma. Drawing upon the early-attachment studies of mothers and infants, researchers tell us that a physical bond between people, as with couples, means an even greater capacity to affect each other's emotions and body states (Schore 2003). Given their conscious and unconscious ties, partners can often regulate each other's emotional experiences with just a glance. On both conscious and unconscious levels, partners alternately validate, enhance, arouse, calm, and soothe each other despite the fact that they may also enrage, disappoint, insult, and aggravate each other. In short, given the bond you share with your partner, your presence is uniquely effective in reducing the assault of trauma.

Sarah and Bill were from very different backgrounds. Married for seven years, they lived in the Northeastern city where Bill had grown up as an only child. Sarah, on the other hand, was the oldest child and only daughter in a family of four from the South.

As Bill knew, Sarah's decision to attend school and remain in the Northeast had been a source of both relief and guilt and a reason for considerable criticism by her family. When Sarah got the call that her parents had been injured in a car accident, Bill decided to go with her to Memphis. He heard her say that he didn't really have to go and that she could manage on her own, but he saw her look of relief when he said he just wanted to go to help out. He had no real experience with big families, but he figured that everyone would be stressed and that, if he could just pick up some meals or help with driving to and from the hospital, it might ease everyone's tension. Knowing that Sarah would be trying to make decisions with brothers who accused her of never being around, he also wanted Sarah to feel like her "team" was there with her. When they flew home after a week, Sarah let Bill know how grateful she was and how his presence had helped her deal with her family. They both understood that having the person you love nearby makes coping a little easier.

The Gift of Containment

When feelings are intense, it is easy to feel overwhelmed and immobilized. This can be frightening and uncomfortable especially for someone unaccustomed to experiencing a high degree of emotion. In these situations, a trusted partner can help contain the feelings, making it possible and safe for the person to express these feelings. Serving as a container for your partner's intense feelings can be done with or without words. Nonverbal connection like a hug or gentle touch when the other is in emotional pain is often experienced as understanding and support. Sometimes, when there are no words, just being together is enough. And when one of you needs to speak, just listening sends a message of care and concern. It means that it is safe and acceptable to express painful feelings.

Just Being There

It is easy to overlook the importance of *just being there* when someone you love is feeling sad or scared and unable or unwilling to give voice to those feelings. Knowing that the person you love is crying can make you feel heartbroken for him or her and helpless. Sometimes you don't know what to say. Sometimes you yourself are so upset that you cannot put feelings into words. It is very important to know that just being there when someone you love is upset is powerful in recovery.

> Carey was hysterical when she learned that her younger brother, just thirty years old, had been diagnosed with late-stage lung cancer. Jack, her husband, was also stunned and not sure how to help. The only thing he could do was listen and hug her. This let Carey know that someone was there to hold her and accept her no matter what she felt.

Active Listening

Often a partner needs to put feelings into words and let them be heard without fear of judgment or upsetting the other. Being there to listen while your partner expresses feelings is also a gift of containment. But this is not easy. In the face of your partner's verbal expression of pain, you may have the urge to *do something*. Active listening is a way of doing something. This technique, first suggested by Carl Rogers (1989), provides safety to the person experiencing pain because the partner who is listening has no goal other than support, warmth, creation of safety, and containment of feelings. Active listening involves putting yourself in the shoes of the speaker. You take in that person's words, tone, and nonverbal expression so that you can grasp his or her point of view and then convey back what you think he or she is saying or feeling.

> While trying to understand her brother's illness, Carey began to repeat, "This can't be true. Who is healthier than my brother? You know him—he never even smoked! What happened? Tell me what you think happened." Feeling the intensity of her pain but knowing he had no answers, Jack held Carey and said, "Carey, I don't know. I hear you—it's too much to believe. He's your brother; I know how much you love him and it just doesn't make sense. It's just too much."

Active listening is not about encouraging, prodding, fixing, or minimizing. It is just listening and verbalizing what you have heard. Often we think we are helping by trying to talk reason, reassuring, or trying to help our partner look forward to a better future. These are not bad things, and trying to help your partner move out of pain is commendable, but healing and recovery from trauma happen in stages. In the early stage of trauma, as was the case with Carey, people often just need to register unimaginable horror. When we rush the person into feeling better, he or she may get the message that these feelings are unacceptable or that what he or she has experienced should not be shared.

> *Charlie stopped counting the number of times Justine described the scene in which she and their baby were hit by another car, the experience of her glasses falling off, and her panic and helplessness at not being able to see what had happened to the baby. Somewhat in shock himself at having come so close to losing his wife and baby, Charlie did not know what to say. Justine was so upset. He was struck with how she couldn't stop talking about it. The best he could do was to actively listen, with responses like "It sounds like a nightmare," "I don't even know what to say," and "I'm hearing how bad it was, Justine. It's so hard to shake the scared feeling." This gave him a way to respond to Justine, to let her know he was trying to understand. It also gave her permission to do what is very common after trauma—verbalize the terrifying moment again and again in order to make sense of it, to find a way to register the horror you are never prepared for.*

Being a compassionate presence can help each of you learn a great deal about your partner's needs and concerns through observing, listening, and containing. We trust that by now you realize that being a compassionate presence does not mean spending hours together or being therapists for each other. It does not mean that you first have to talk about the trauma, the injury, the baby, or the war. Rather, since trauma may have left you feeling like you can't find a way back to how you were before the disruptive event, it may mean simply feeling the presence of each other and recognizing the value of your connection.

Principle 2: Establishing Physical and Psychological Safety

Most of us spend our lives feeling reasonably safe in the world we have created. We feel positive about ourselves and we enjoy predictability and meaning in our routines and in the world around us. For the individual who has experienced trauma, the world has changed and the sense of safety is lost. Because the mind-body connection is very powerful in allowing the person to register this loss of safety, one of the healthiest things we can do is to reduce the degree and duration of stress on our bodies and our minds.

Physical Safety: Taking Care of Basic Needs

It is common in the aftermath of trauma and disaster for the body to continue to brace itself for danger, even though you have literally moved out of harm's way—the hurricane has passed, the funeral is over, your deployment cycle has ended. In a sense, your body remains on alert, ready for fight or flight, often fueled by memories or intrusive images. Bessel van der Kolk (1996a, 214), noted traumatologist, tells us that "the body keeps score." For this reason, when establishing safety, we begin with the body.

When working with couples who have faced trauma, we always ask, "Are you sleeping? Are you eating? What are you doing to relax?" It is not uncommon for those faced with a traumatic event to neglect their basic human needs. Not eating properly or not eating at all; not sleeping at night; overusing sleep aids, cigarettes, and caffeine; and overlooking exercise and rest are frequent companions to traumatic stress symptoms.

Resetting the Body's Rhythms

Resetting the body's rhythms, like resetting a circuit breaker, is crucial in the recovery from trauma, and partners may be able to support each other in this process. Among military and uniformed service personnel who face traumatic events as part of their mission, "buddy care" is the way that comrades keep an eye out for each other's basic needs. In a similar way, we recommend that couples practice "partner care." This means gently keeping an eye on your partner's sleeping, eating, and relaxing habits. Why *gently*? One of the vicious traps in the body's reaction to trauma is the tendency to overreact to the disruption. For example, stress disrupts sleep and disrupted sleep physiologically creates more stress. Panic about not sleeping or vigilance by one's partner ratchets up the stress and rarely brings forth a good night's sleep. Instead of being vigilant or using directives, you can observe disruptions or changes in your and your partner's body rhythms, with the goal of helping each other ease back into healthier patterns.

> *Hank and Lisa, a couple whom we met in one of our workshops, reported that, since the death of their son on 9/11, they were both having trouble sleeping. Hank would generally fall asleep in front of the TV. When he woke up a while later he would head to bed, only to find that he couldn't sleep. Lisa was having difficulty because during the quiet time of the night she would think of her son, get upset, and then be unable to fall asleep. Exhausted, she began to push sleep as late as possible, only to awaken early in the morning. Both were irritable, tired, and judgmental of the other's sleep problem. It helped Hank and Lisa to hear that, though keeping an eye on sleep is very important, obsessing about sleep or blaming someone for their sleep disturbance never helps.*

Strategy: Partner Care for Sleeping Patterns

1. **Take an interest in each other.** Instead of watching each other with worry and concern, consider watching with tender (even lighthearted) mutual interest. Ask each other, "How are you doing?"

2. **Observe yourself.** Before discussing the issue of sleep, ask yourself if you are getting the same amount of sleep that you have in the past. If not, are you having a difficult time falling asleep? Are you falling asleep but waking very early? Are you finding that you are sleeping more than ever, or that you feel exhausted all the time?

3. **Reframe your perspective by recognizing the following:**

* Sleep disruption is normal given the circumstances.

* Trauma and grieving are exhausting—you might be tired even if you are getting your usual amount of sleep.

* Sleep problems can be solved.

* Exercise and physical activity will help you reset your sleep pattern. Whether you jog, go to a gym, or simply walk around your neighborhood, you can change your body's pattern. If you can't walk, try some physical activity, be it vacuuming or sweeping the garage. This can help your hyperaroused body do what it is wired to do in the face of trauma—*move*.

4. **Try something different.**

* Distractions such as watching TV can help to interrupt your ruminating about the trauma and assist with falling asleep.

* When you are trying to fall asleep, make *relaxing* rather than sleeping the initial goal, and set up new rituals for relaxing before sleep.

* To reduce the fear of waking and not falling back to sleep, plan something to do until you feel sleepy again, in the event that you do wake up (read, snack, write, pray, watch TV, and so on).

5. **Be creative and collaborative in solving sleep problems.**

* Can you use a book light so as not to disturb your partner?

* Can you accept that your partner may need to get up a few times during the night for a while?

* Would it help to move a TV into or out of the bedroom?

* Would you consider putting the TV on a timer?

- Do you or does your partner have interest in mutual relaxation or romance?

- Can you take turns sleeping late in the morning while the other deals with the children, pets, or other responsibilities?

- Does one of you need to sleep in another room for a while?

6. **Consider medication.** One or both of you may want to consider talking to a doctor regarding medication if you are unable to sleep, your sleep is continually disrupted by traumatic nightmares, or your overall functioning (your ability to work, care for children, drive, or think clearly) is impaired or jeopardized by continued sleep problems.

It goes without saying that loss of appetite, overeating, and stress eating dovetail with insomnia, exhaustion, and emotional stress.

Lisa had no interest in eating, much less cooking, after losing her son. Even though friends and neighbors often brought food to them, Hank could see that Lisa was not eating. Besides worrying about her, he missed the couple time they had always shared over Lisa's home-cooked meals. In an attempt to help both of them, Hank decided to try his hand at cooking dinners. He tried making things like spinach omelets and grilled burgers, and he would ask Lisa how he had done. Touched and amused that he was trying to cook for them, Lisa was willing to join him and eat some, even just to thank him for his effort. In a sense, they were giving each other partner care.

Strategy: Partner Care for Eating Patterns

1. **Start with self-care.** There is so much focus on and sensitivity around eating in this culture that it may be best to start by considering yourself: Are you eating? Overeating? Do you have any appetite?

Most people are surviving the best they can in the aftermath of trauma. In most cases, they get their appetite back and address any problems with overeating. By taking care of yourself, you model healthy behavior to a partner who is not eating or is overeating. More important, taking care of yourself also reduces the stress on a worried partner and makes you better able to help your partner if needed.

2. **Create informal opportunities.** Inviting positive opportunities to eat together can be a way of helping your partner. If being together is healing and desirable, what you are eating, be it a snack or a dinner, is of less importance. It's possible that eating together on a regular basis will awaken your or your partner's appetite. It is just as valuable when a partner invites the other to keep him or her company during a meal or snack, whether they both plan to eat or not.

3. **Think differently about eating.** If you or your partner becomes aware that you are overeating, it is worth asking yourself: Are you really exhausted and eating to stay awake? Are you eating rather than feeling? Do you have other opportunities for dealing with these feelings? Are you eating as a way to try to lower the agitation and stress that come after trauma?

4. **Use stress-reducing activities.** If you have discovered that eating or not eating is an attempt to deal with stress-related feelings, trying activities that reduce stress can be useful.

Using Stress-Reducing Activities

The impact of trauma is often more a function of whether or not a person has a stress-reducing activity or ritual in place than the actual degree of the traumatic event.

Hank described that in the aftermath of losing his son he was "without words." He really didn't want to be with other people. He appreciated their efforts but felt that there was nothing he

*could say. What helped him cope was spending time working
in his garden. While he was tending his plants, his mind could
go anywhere. He didn't have to be strong and he didn't have to
revisit the loss for the sake of someone else's concern.*

*Lisa had more difficulty than Hank did. Reading had
always been a favorite pastime for her, but now she just could
not get through a page. Desperate, she tried to return to sewing,
but she could not concentrate on that either. She felt as if she had
lost her safe escapes. Finally, someone recommended that she try
walking to help improve her sleep patterns, and this worked. It
became a new and actually enjoyable stress reliever for her. When
Hank joined her with an interest in looking at other people's
gardens, it became a new experience for both of them to share.*

Strategy: Partner Care for Relaxation and Stress Reduction

A partner's recognition, respect, and reinforcement of the other's relaxation and stress-reducing activities are a great asset in recovery from trauma. A stress-reducing activity need not be a formal yoga class or new sport. Actually, the best stress-reducing activity is a small and predictable activity that generally creates a good feeling. The routine of reading the paper, doing the daily crossword, listening to the radio, playing the piano, sitting with a cup of coffee in a favorite chair—all of these qualify as stress-free times when your body and mind relax, even for a few minutes.

1. **Start with the familiar.** People are often so thrown or frozen after a traumatic event that they don't recognize the benefit of resuming some of their familiar rituals. As soon as you can, return to your small stress-reducing activities and encourage your partner to do the same.

2. **Give each other permission.** People often feel as if they are "on hold" until their loved one is out of the hospital or life is back to normal. Sometimes people feel guilty enjoying even small aspects of their life if others have lost their lives or have sustained greater injury or loss of resources. Balancing your grief or empathy for others with

relaxing, stress-reducing moments for yourself is a health-promoting and important part of your recovery.

3. **Try something new.** As Lisa discovered, if none of your old stress relievers seem possible, try something new. You can invite your partner to do the same. Learning something new often helps relieve stress because, while you are trying to knit, play a new card game, learn how to use the computer, or refinish furniture, you are usually not able to think of anything else.

Overall, you can both share partner care for basic needs, whether one or both have been directly exposed to a traumatic event. It is important to remember, as you keep an eye on each other, that you are aiming to reinstitute a feeling of control of yourself as part of your efforts to establish safety. This is difficult to do if all basic needs are provided by one partner or if you feel nagged to meet needs for yourself. The idea is mutual support and care.

Psychological Safety: Creating a Safe Space

Isolation and alienation have often been described as common psychological experiences in the aftermath of trauma. Essentially these unfold from the inability to grasp what has happened. The feeling of isolation comes with the sudden disconnection from a familiar self and a familiar world. After a traumatic event, even if surrounded by crowds, a person may have the sense that one is alone—the feeling of being different from others, of never being the same as other people again. Because of this, it has been found that human connection, particularly familiar networks of support, is the most crucial element in the early response to trauma (Ørner 2004).

We also know that the quality of the initial contact can play an important part in the subsequent reactions to the traumatic event. If a person feels supported and cared for by others in the early hours after the event, there is a greater chance that he or she will seek connection in the days and months that follow (Shalev 2005). The very fact that you are a couple, that you have each other, adds to the psychological safety you need during and after the experience of trauma. Even being able to call or e-mail a partner gives you a built-in initial contact. This connection reduces the feeling that trauma often brings of being completely alone.

Normalizing Reactions (Experiencing Normal Reactions to Abnormal Events)

Normalizing your own and your partner's feelings and behavior in response to the trauma is crucial to creating psychological safety. It is difficult to feel safe in a psychological sense if you are worried that your feelings, fears, thoughts, or behaviors seem abnormal or crazy. Likewise, if you are similarly worried about your partner, you will have a harder time feeling safe within your relationship.

So what is a "normal" reaction to trauma? Trauma responses are normal responses to abnormal events. It is common to feel shaken, have sleep problems, and be easily triggered to feel anxiety or grief by a sight, sound, or smell. Knowing that these reactions are normal does not mean that you are expected to be comfortable with them, but knowing that they are common reactions may help you feel less worried and better prepared to deal with them.

No matter what trauma you have suffered, remember that *it is the event itself that is abnormal; your reactions and those of your partner, while perhaps radically different from each other, are normal attempts to cope.*

Lowering Stress Through Information

A major stress reliever in the aftermath of trauma and disaster is to have or receive correct and appropriate information, whether it is the name of a shelter where you can bring your family or the treatment plan suggested in dealing with an injured child. Because traumas are by nature unexpected and out of the realm of one's usual experience, they leave people feeling confused and unable to grasp what is happening. Because the mind and body are connected, when people intellectually know what is going on or what to expect, they feel less anxious and more in control physically. You can use couples psychological first aid when you provide information to each other as well as supporting each other in dealing with the information given. Doug and Ginny's situation is an example of this.

When Doug and Ginny got the late-night call telling them that their daughter had been in a car accident, Ginny was quietly thankful that Doug could drive and follow the directions given to the hospital. She did not hear a word anyone said after hearing her daughter was seriously hurt. Later that day, their roles were reversed when she was able to take in everything the doctors said and explain it to Doug, who by that time was on emotional overload. The fact that they could take turns receiving and providing the information was an invaluable way of lowering each other's anxiety and offering each other support.

Changing Perceptions

As you gain more understanding of traumatic reactions, your understanding of how they affect your relationship will increase. Gradually your perceptions are likely to change. You may begin to take each other's reactions less personally and with less pain. For example, if you know your partner is not sleeping much, seeing his irritability as fatigue rather than dissatisfaction with you may reduce your own defensive anger and increase your tolerance. If he understands your withdrawal and unwillingness to talk about the recent tragedy as a mode of self-protection and an attempt to feel less vulnerable, then he will be less likely to feel rejected. These shifts in perception may assist each of you in being a more compassionate presence for the other.

When Carl returned from his eighteen-month assignment in the military, he seemed cautious and distant. He stayed awake long after Maria said good night and seemed unapproachable when she just wanted to talk or spend time together. She was relieved that Carl had decided to speak to someone at the local readjustment center, which provided counseling for combat veterans, but she felt personally helpless and feared that their relationship would never be the same. Feeling like she needed more information, she started attending programs offered at that same center for spouses of combat vets. Hearing other wives talk about the reactions of their newly returned husbands and reading through the material reduced some of her fears that there might be something wrong with her and Carl. She saw that many couples were also facing readjustments to married and family life. Understanding more about trauma changed her reactions. Her ability to understand hyperarousal and the triggers of traumatic memory as well as the healing and recovery process helped her feel less worried and improved her relationship with Carl in a number of ways.

One of the ways was her ability to recognize the effects of trauma triggers on Carl. When she heard a car backfire one day, Maria saw Carl brace himself and look away. When he looked back at her with some embarrassment, Maria reached out and touched his hand. She said, "You know, at the center they were talking about how common it is to react to noises. It makes sense." Carl was quiet, and then he said, "Yeah, a lot of guys talk about it." This happened a few times, and finally Carl said, "It is just not easy to forget." Maria just responded, "Yeah, I'm glad you are home." Maria began to understand why even some of the normal sounds of life with three children in a small house were difficult and disturbing for Carl. Though she was not about to ask the children to stop having fun, shut off the music, or turn friends away, she explained to him that she could understand his reactions. She let him know that she recognized, when he spent time in his workroom, that it was not necessarily to get away from her but to get some quiet, safe time. This expression of understanding got them talking more and improved the feeling between them.

Another way Maria's changed perceptions helped their relationship was in the area of allowing time for healing. She felt like she had been turning down invitations to socialize with friends for such a long time, but she knew from Carl's hesitation that he was still not ready to socialize much with their group of neighbors and friends. She admitted to herself how much she missed the social aspect of their life together, but she knew that he was working on this at the readjustment center. She could see small changes that allowed her to hope that what they were facing would not last forever. By seeing this as a trauma-related situation, Maria and Carl were able to discuss social invitations with less anger and resentment. There was less pressure and more flexibility in their decisions about whether both or one of them would attend. Accepting a realistic time period for *healing lowered the tension as they worked their way back to a social life they both could enjoy.*

Strategy: Shifting Partner Perceptions

People often protect themselves by assuming the worst. This is one of the traps that couples fall into after trauma. Negative perceptions often escalate a spiral of negative assumptions that create the very thing that is feared. In other words, if you assume that your partner is rejecting you rather than using time and space to lower anxiety, then you may react to your assumption and spark the rejection you fear.

1. **Open the possibilities.** Instead of perceiving your partner's behavior in a negative light, consider saying to yourself, "I'm not sure what my partner is feeling." Assuming that you don't know is a valuable stop sign for negative projections and predictions. It is often the first step toward actually knowing what your partner feels.

2. **Remind yourself of the context.** Take into account that you are both experiencing the emotional fallout of a traumatic event. The behaviors you observe in each other are most likely related to what you have faced. This does not mean that they are not upsetting or that you should ignore them. Putting them into context, however, is likely to alter the way you feel and how you address them. The examples of couples handling common trauma reactions in chapter 1 provide an insider view of this type of situation.

3. **Connect with your partner in a different way to get a new perspective.** Instead of asking why your partner looks depressed or upset, suggest you both take a quick ride for a cup of coffee or walk the dog together. The more experience you have as a couple in informal, positive, everyday exchanges, the more you will have a chance to recapture familiar feelings as well as take some new steps beyond the trauma.

4. **Allow time for healing.** Remind yourself, as Maria did in the last example, that healing and recovery take place in small steps over time.

Exercise: Understanding Your Couple Coping Style

Just as individuals have a characteristic way of responding to stress, so too do couples. Take a moment to think about mildly stressful times earlier in your relationship. Perhaps you recall that at such times you really pulled together as a team for support and problem solving and you are confident that you will be able to do that again. On the other hand, you may remember that at times of stress you both had less tolerance for minor annoyances or that each of you dealt with the tension by moving apart and seeking distraction in the form of work or exercise. That method of dealing with stress may very well emerge in an exaggerated fashion now. Remember, you have probably not faced anything like this before. Finally, it's possible that your reaction in the face of this trauma may feel uncharacteristic of your relationship. Don't be alarmed. While this may feel frightening, it is not an indication that you will not be able to work through it. It simply means that you need to realize the impact of what has happened, be aware of how it unfolds, and use resources such as the suggestions offered here to maximize your couple coping potential.

Following are a few questions to think about. Feel free to write down your answers in a notebook or in the Notes section at the end of the book, and invite your partner to do the same.

- Are you able to recognize the stimuli that trigger reactions in either yourself or your partner?

- Can you alter the triggers or your reaction to them?

- Does each of you give yourself permission to take care of your individual needs when your partner is just not able to respond?

- Do you often find yourselves on opposite sides of an issue rather than joining forces to creatively solve the problem? Can you think about changing this?

- Are you as patient with the recovery process as you would like to be?

- Can you begin to use your expanding knowledge of the impact of trauma to increase patience and tolerance?

Principle 3: Identifying and Responding to Needs

Understanding what each of you needs and what you need as a couple in the aftermath of trauma is important but not easy. You may feel so far away from your former life and your former self that it is difficult to know what you need, much less what your partner needs. Your partner's behaviors that in the past might have seemed comforting and desirable may now create stress. Perhaps your partner has always asked about your day or inquired what time you are coming home; these inquiries may now seem intrusive or unwelcome. In the early stages of trauma, trying to understand and communicate needs can help partners feel safer and more stable.

Using a Feeling-Need-Response Style

Sometimes it's difficult to figure out what your needs even are. When working with couples who are trying to communicate their needs to their partner, we have told each partner, "If you can identify what you are feeling, it will be easier to recognize your need." Here are some examples of feelings and their related needs:

I feel hungry.   I need to eat.

I feel lonely.   I need to be with someone.

I feel shaky.   I need to sit down.

Once you recognize your need, you can choose to do the following:

- **Respond to it yourself.** "I feel hungry. I need to eat. I will make a sandwich."

- **Communicate the feeling and need to your partner with an I-message.** "I feel hungry. I need to eat." By sending this message, you offer your partner the opportunity to participate in a number of ways. He or she may offer to cook, suggest some particular food, or join in a discussion with you about it.

- **Make a request accompanied by an I-message.** "I feel hungry. I need to eat. Can we go have a sandwich?" When a request is made with an I-message that includes the feeling and the need, it is often very effective because it provides a partner with the reason behind a request. When a partner understands the need, the request is experienced with more empathy.

Thomas Gordon (1970) coined the terms *you-messages* and *I-messages* in his work on parent effectiveness training. You will see throughout this book that using an I-message is a very effective way of communicating with a partner because it gives a partner information that he or she does not already have. As we look more closely at identifying and responding to needs, you will see that the use of an I-message is effective even with less concrete needs and often invites the compassionate presence and active listening that we described earlier. For example, "I've been thinking a lot about Joe lately and how he was killed" may make the veteran realize "I need to be alone for a while." This invites a partner to understand, and perhaps simply say, "I'm so sorry about Joe. I'm here if you need me." Compare this with the common "I need to be alone for a while," leading to the typical response "You never want to spend time with me." You can see why stating the feeling (the I-message) along with the need is much more effective.

Recognizing Changes in Needs and Roles

In the aftermath of trauma, things are going to be different. Often, the balance that you previously enjoyed—the equilibrium between meeting the needs of both partners and meeting the needs of the relationship—is somewhat off center. If each of you feels that your personal resources are being stretched thin, it may seem like you have little left to give to one another. Acknowledging this, and realigning your priorities and expectations, can help tremendously. Don't be afraid to make a change in who does what, when, and how often. Once a couple makes a plan to pull together to get through the traumatic times, they can usually make it work if they feel the connection with the other and respect each other's needs.

We have seen this happen with first responders and their spouses following major emergencies. For example, in the aftermath of 9/11, as traumatized, grief-stricken firefighters focused on the recovery work at the World Trade Center site, their partners and spouses picked up the slack at home while their own needs and the needs of the relationships for the most part went unmentioned. Seen often in military couples, this type of arrangement is not uncommon when trauma directly involves and affects one partner more than the other. We have found in our work that most partners step up with love and pride, putting their own needs aside to support the mission.

The caution for both partners is that when needs go unexpressed and unmet, with time they can become the seeds of resentment. The partner at home can be so worried about the partner in the hospital or in Iraq that she doesn't express her understandable wish to be recognized for what she has done to "hold it all together." The partner who has been away is often so overwhelmed that he has simply not realized what has happened while he was gone. Sometimes, on returning home, he might see that his partner has done so much while he was away that he feels guilty, even useless. Often the way back is for couples to show appreciation for what each has been through: "I couldn't have done it without you—how do I help you now that I am home?" or "Did you know that wherever you were, I was standing behind you?" These are statements of recognition and reconnection. This recognition helps couples to move on as a team.

Fear of Being Selfish

An important underlying message of couples psychological first aid is that the stability of a couple is equal to the sum of its parts. Even in situations in which the trauma has directly affected both partners, as with the loss of child or home, it is important for each of you to think about your individual needs. Too often we hear folks express the opinion that thinking about their own needs rather than the needs of their partner is selfish or uncaring. Not so! In fact, in suggesting the use of couples psychological first aid, we hope that each of you will recognize and satisfy your own needs in a way that helps strengthen your relationship.

Strategy: Clarity and Care of Your Own Needs

After trauma, partners are often afraid to step away from each other to meet their own needs. Beginning to do things for and by yourself can be helpful to both of you. If you realize that you feel stressed or lonely, for example, you might ask yourself, "What do I need to do that will help me without posing a risk or threat to my relationship?" You may feel a need to exercise, to be with your buddies, or to see a movie. There's no need for a lengthy discussion or negotiation, just a clear I-message regarding your feeling, need, and plan. I-messages such as "I'm feeling kind of stressed. I think I need some time with my friends. I'm going to see that chick flick with the girls," "I really need some time to exercise," and "I think I need to spend some time with my brothers" actually become very important communications and actions.

Perhaps you feel you are already doing too much by and for yourself. What about the things you want or need from your partner? Here, you might begin by asking yourself, "What do I really need from my partner and how will I communicate it without risk of making things worse?" You may find an answer to this question in recognizing and understanding differences.

Recognizing and Understanding Differences

People heal in different ways and according to different timelines. How you grieve or respond to trauma may be a function of who you are, your age, your gender, and the circumstances of your loss. Typically, though not always, if you are female, you may want to talk with others—and maybe for a while you can't stop talking about the loss. If you are male, you may want to do anything but talk. (Of course we have also seen this gender pattern in reverse.) What is rare is for partners to have identical ways of handling the emotional overload they may be feeling. Accepting what the other needs is part of the recovery for both. How you think about your partner and the meaning of his or her behavior can make a difference in how you feel in response to it.

Again, it may help to remember that in times of crisis most of us are who we are—and more. Behaviors that were somewhat problematic early on in the relationship may return in times of crisis. You may find that your partner is once again unable to express his feelings or that you are clingy and tearful when your partner leaves for work. It can help to recognize these as temporary setbacks related to the trauma that are likely to shift again with time.

> Joan and Tom had faced Joan's diagnosis and surgery for breast cancer together. Despite the good prognosis her doctors had given her, however, Joan and Tom were having a hard time settling back into life. It upset Joan that no matter what she said and what plans she suggested Tom did not seem interested and would go off by himself. Initially this was both perplexing and disturbing to her—just as she was feeling better and wanting to put it all behind her, Tom seemed to avoid her. Sometimes she would notice that when he was playing with their three-year-old his eyes would fill with tears and he would go into another room so as not to upset her. Feeling guilty for all the worry she had caused him but impatient to go on with their lives and spend time together, Joan began to bring a magazine into the TV room when he was watching sports and silently sit next to him. When he looked at her with an expression that said, "What's up?" she would smile and say, "Just want to hang out." Realizing that he was still reacting to the possibility of losing her, she was gently sending the nonverbal message, "It's okay; we have both been through a lot." Sometimes she asked him what was going on with the game; sometimes she jokingly tried to push him off the sofa. Sometimes he would laugh despite himself, and sometimes his eyes would

well up, but he did not run away. Joan's reassuring presence said
to him, "We can heal together." With time, Tom began to express
more and actually seemed to enjoy her hanging out with him. Joan
had found a way to express her needs without overlooking his.

As part of a couple, your path and goals for recovery are different than they would be if you were alone. Even as you try to understand your partner's needs or communicate your own, you want to also take into account those decisions that will foster the healing of your relationship.

Restoring the Spirit of "We"

In every couple's relationship, there is an "I," a "you," and a "we," each with distinct needs. Most couples find that preserving the "we," that unique combination and joint identification that makes them a couple, is crucial in their recovery. This may mean that at times you will each decide to do things because you are aware that it will benefit the "we"—both of you as a couple.

After trauma, one partner may feel the need to support the relationship sooner or more sharply than the other. It is helpful to communicate this to your partner while making clear that you are not making a demand and don't want to create additional stress. As with Joan and Tom, sometimes one partner can respond to an overture of closeness long before he could possibly initiate it.

When the "we" seems to be slipping away, it is important to actually make a plan that allows you to feel the connection of being together. Taking steps to be in the same physical space can be a precursor to making a date for coffee, ice cream, or a hamburger. Don't be afraid to be the initiator, to explain how you are feeling, and express why you are trying to make a plan for being together. Let your partner know that you understand that he or she may not yet feel a need for this, but that you are hoping to work out something comfortable for both of you. As long as you are reasonable and willing to be both flexible and patient, both of you will benefit.

What Words Can't Say

Talking is only one way to express needs and concerns. Researchers tell us that we can detect and process the smallest change in a human face within one hundred milliseconds (Lehky 2000)—that is, at levels beneath our awareness. When people are intimately connected they are particularly interested in and aware of each other's nonverbal cues (Schore 2003). Often, a partner knows when the other is stressed because of something very subtle, such as a look others might not notice, or because he or she observes the other overeating, drinking too much, becoming very quiet, sleeping during the day, cleaning, coming home late, avoiding sex, or complaining of physical pain or discomfort.

You don't want to make your partner feel self-conscious by pointing out expressions of pain, sadness, guilt, and the like. No one wants to live under a microscope or to be constantly *analyzed* by their partner. On the other hand, what you observe in your partner may reflect something that he or she needs or something that interferes with your need. Understanding each other in a nonverbal way may be even more important now as one or both of you struggle with the impact of the trauma.

After Cheryl lost the baby, she stopped saying much and didn't seem to want to do anything. Nick saw her expression when they were in the company of friends with kids, but was unsure if he should say anything. Around the house, he would try to engage her but she was always busy with chores. As a few months went by, Nick worried that they would both fall into despair. He wanted to make his need for time and connection with Cheryl clear, so he started leaving little notes asking her for a date. Cheryl threw them away or ignored them. Trying not to feel rejected, Nick started leaving larger notes. Each day the note on the refrigerator got larger until finally he taped up a piece of tagboard that said, "You're my girl—I won't give up. How about dinner Friday night?" They settled on a lunch date.

Strategy: Utilize What You Observe

Following are some tips for putting your observations to use as you work to meet your needs and the needs of your relationship:

■ If you choose to respond to what you have observed, be a natural and compassionate presence. For example, if you see that your partner looks uncomfortable at a party, ask whether he wants to stay. If he says yes, you might want to remain near him. If your partner looks upset when reading something in the paper, ask if he wants to talk about it; if not, offer a loving touch or hug. If your partner is clearly upset about something that happened at work, give him space and see if he begins talking about it.

■ If your partner's behavior interferes with your need, try to understand what is happening. For example, if every time you start to share your worry about the future your partner walks away and leaves the room, you may need to ask yourself, "What am I feeling? Why do I need to speak to her about my worries? Am I pushing her away without realizing it? Perhaps she is unable to deal with the future at this time. Perhaps I never speak about anything but worries or complaints and she is saturated. Should I see if we can regain some connection by talking about other things as a first step?"

■ If you feel confused and unable to get a sense of what your partner is feeling, share your confusion, rather than trying to guess what's wrong. It may be helpful to remind your partner that you can be a listening ear. If sharing is too much for your partner or listening is too much for you, consider seeking the help of a mental health professional. Often this takes the pressure off both partners. Just knowing that there are helpers out there can make sharing and listening together easier.

Some Thoughts on Needs

We hope that the previous examples have served to demonstrate that there are many ways to navigate difficult situations with your partner. At times you may do things because you need to, at other times because your partner needs you to, and at still others because it is in the best interest of your relationship. There will be times when your needs may be trumped by your fear of upsetting your partner. There will be times when your needs will clash. However, as you begin to identify your needs more clearly and communicate them more effectively, each of you will learn to listen to both the words and the feelings being communicated and begin to see alternatives that can give you hope for the future.

Principle 4: Offering Practical Assistance and Enhancing Positive Coping Skills

In the aftermath of trauma, people are often unable to concentrate or focus their attention on the tasks they usually perform with relative ease. The reason for this is that, at the time of a traumatic event, the "thinking" part of the brain shuts down in order to optimize the fight-or-flight response you need to handle a high-stress situation. The resulting *cognitive fog* can be disruptive to both the individual and the couple attempting to reestablish their normal routines.

Stepping Up and Stepping Back

If you or your partner is having difficulty focusing on reading, dealing with bills, keeping to a schedule, or remembering to take care of many of the details of daily living, it can be simultaneously frightening and annoying to both of you. We believe that understanding the reasons for such lapses can help partners to feel better about stepping up and filling in when they see something left unattended. Seeing these shifts in routine as temporary and recognizing that they are appreciated by your partner can go a long way toward your ability to see recovery as a shared endeavor. Here is how one couple put this principle into action:

Alice returned to work a week after her mom was killed in a car accident. Although she appeared to be doing okay there, at home she seemed unable to focus on anything. It was as if going to work took all her energy. She had always been great at keeping the bills organized and paid on time; now they were piling up and she was unable to check on the kids' homework, tend to the house, or make dinner. Without saying much, Joe mentioned that he would pick up the bill paying and help with the kids and dinners for a while. While they didn't talk about it, his help did not go unnoticed or unappreciated. Alice began to relax and feel less stressed and guilty for not doing as much as she previously had.

Sometimes you may realize that your partner needs you to step back—when she or he needs space, solitude, and a reduction in stimuli. For many partners, stepping back is more difficult, since it is often in direct opposition to their own need for contact and connection.

Fostering Connection with Social Support Systems

There is ample evidence that the most important resource people need in the aftermath of trauma is connection to their family and existing social support systems (Ørner 2004). This is why your relationship has the potential to be the most important healing element in your recovery. Those reeling in the aftermath of trauma, however, may first seek comfort from others who have shared their traumatic experience. This may explain why a firefighter needs to be with his "brothers" when grieving the death of a young firefighter, even if he did not personally know him. It may explain why a woman might feel she needs to speak more to her mother and sisters after a miscarriage or why the returning veteran is e-mailing his buddies in Iraq. You may at first feel threatened if your partner turns to others rather than to you when suffering and in pain. After all, you are the one who is there "for better or for worse," standing by wanting only to understand and to help. This "trauma membrane," as it is called, sometimes forms around those who have shared an unspeakable experience; understanding this concept may help you recognize that your partner's need to be with others need not threaten your primary relationship (Lindy 1986). In fact, healing in community with others who have suffered in a similar way facilitates recovery.

Supporting your partner may mean supporting or helping him or her to connect with others who can provide support that you can't. This action recognizes that we all need multiple support systems, especially during our most stressful times. Turning to friends and family can supplement your available resources and enhance both partners' ability to maintain needed energy over the long haul. Be careful not to think of support from a partner and support from other social sources as separate or different. By working as a team you can sometimes bring these resources together, for the benefit of all.

Steven and Brenda found a way to combine support resources after Brenda's sister died of cancer. Steven wanted to help and began to pick up the slack at home while Brenda spent almost every night getting dinner for her four nephews. Steven knew that it was her way of staying close to her sister, but still he started feeling like he was the one who had lost his wife. Brenda felt bad about this but had no answers—she missed her sister terribly and felt that if she had been the one who died, her sister would have been there for Steven and their children. Tension between Brenda and Steven began to build. It was only when Steven got involved with his nephews and his brother-in-law and encouraged Brenda to invite them back to their house that the tension began to ease. Both seemed relieved as they started facing the crisis as a team.

Knowing How and When to Use Professional Help

Offering assistance to each other also means finding out when it is time to get more help. Often, one partner is the "researcher" in the family, looking things up on the Internet or consulting others to find community resources, doctors, support groups, and so on. Sometimes after a trauma, both partners share the task of investigating options— for example, one of you may have purchased this book and brought it to the other's attention.

Education is a powerful tool for helping you to understand what is happening—as long as you don't assume that everything that *may* happen *will* happen. Especially when one partner has taken the lead in learning about the signs and symptoms of trauma, it is important not to become hypervigilant—assuming, for example, that every one of your partner's reactions constitutes evidence of hyperarousal or avoidance.

With this caution in mind, you can work as a team to determine when self-help is no longer enough (see chapter 3). There may be times when consulting a professional makes sense. Maybe you and your partner are so sleep deprived that you find it difficult to make it through the day, or your concentration is so poor that you cannot get your work done. Perhaps reactivity and irritability are so high that you are concerned about the possibility of road rage or the impact on your children. If you have used the advice we have offered, but the symptoms have persisted for some time and you're not sure you can tolerate them any longer, it may be time to get an expert opinion. A brief period of medication and/ or professional therapy for one or both of you may help restore your functioning so that you can continue to recover as a couple.

Strategy: Practicing the Positives

One way to stock your couple's psychological first aid kit is to practice some of the strategies, like just being there, active listening, partner care, and identifying needs at low-stress, neutral, and even positive times. The benefits of practicing these skills include:

- It is easier to learn a strategy or skill at a low-stress time.

- If these strategies become part of the fabric of your relationship, you will be more likely to utilize them during the painful moments.

- Noticing and celebrating each other's triumphs is a natural buffer for dealing with crisis.

With this in mind, try out the following:

- **Just being there.** The next time your partner forgets his or her cell phone at the office, go along for the ride to pick it up. If one of you is excited to buy an item on sale at a local store, plant some bulbs in the garden, try out a new recipe, or polish the car, just go along and *be there* with your partner for a while.

- **Active listening.** Pick a certain night of the week and decide that on that night, at dinner, before bed, or while taking a walk, each will take a turn sharing something positive that has happened. The other partner will *actively listen to the positive*—listening to the words, tone, and nonverbal expressions of positive feelings. When you are the listener, put yourself in your partner's shoes and then let him or her know what you have heard. For example, you might say, "That's great. I can see how excited you are to have gotten such great seats at the game for you and your friends," or "You made the deal! Oh, that's too good. You sound so proud—you deserve it."

- **Partner care.** Practicing partner care at positive times means observing when your partner is taking good care of him- or herself in an effort to reset the body's rhythms after trauma, by sleeping, eating, and doing stress-reducing activities. For example, you might say, "You are looking so great from all the walking you are doing," or "One thing about you—you really know how to calm down by going to that piano. It's great."

- **Identifying and responding to needs.** Share in fulfilling some noncrucial need your partner has, just because this is a person you love. For example, see the "chick flick" with her. Go to the car dealership with him, just to look around. Pick up a cup of the coffee he likes or the CD she was talking about.

- **If you see something, say something.** Keep your eye out for the positives as a way to reinforce positive coping skills. So, if you notice that he really is a good cook or she is really a great driver, say something. If you know she can help the kids with their homework in a way you can't or if you know he keeps your social life going, say something. If you had a wonderful time or a funny experience together, remind the other so you both store it as a positive memory.

Summary

As you have read, discussed, and practiced the principles of couples psychological first aid, you may have realized that you actually already use some of them. Remember that recovery from trauma is not an event. It is a process. Couples psychological first aid is a part of that process. It involves small, sometimes subtle ways to feel connected; cared for; safer; and more human, normal, and loved. As you proceed with your journey and learn more strategies, revisit the strategies in this chapter frequently—using, improving, changing, and trying out steps in the day-to-day aspects of your relationship. You will see how important these steps are in the next chapter as we take on the question raised by so many of the partners in the aftermath of trauma: "Am I the only one who is angry?"

3

Is Anyone Else Angry?

A love that has endured episodic aggression has a depth and resilience obtainable in no other way.

—Stephen Mitchell (2002)

Anger is a common and complex aspect of trauma. It has a significant impact on a couple's response and recovery. However, it is the nature of intimacy and privacy that leads partners to hide their anger toward their spouse from the outside world—and sometimes even from each other. When we met with small groups of men and women after they had experienced trauma, they often began to talk about their anger. They were frequently perplexed and upset by their feeling and wanted to know, "Is anyone else angry?" Often they wondered, "Why is he nice to outsiders but angry with me and the kids?" or "I know she's angry, but she doesn't say anything, so I'm not really sure why."

Understanding and Changing Anger

In this chapter we will try to answer questions about anger. In our experience, the more partners are able to understand the interplay between anger and trauma, the more they are able to step back from the triggers that are actually more related to the trauma than to each other. We know that when people begin to pay attention to their behavior, and are able to consider and understand the possible causes, they can alter and change their actions.

In this chapter, you will learn that in the aftermath of trauma anger can be tripped by many sources and can reflect different things. It may be, for example, that new expectations of yourself and your partner have led to disappointments, which are expressed as anger, or that erupting anger is actually the result of grief, pain, anxiety, or frustration. You will see that sometimes angry lashing-out at a partner is actually meant for someone else—a family member, the doctor, the army—but it is being misdirected. It is for reasons like these that you may find yourself in the middle of an argument and suddenly realize that you don't even know why you are fighting or how it got started.

We believe that, once you come to recognize the impact of traumatic events on your life and how feelings like heightened anxiety can trigger anger, you may realize that you are more upset about what has happened than with each other. We want you to understand anger in a way that helps you redefine it, defuse it, and use it as a point of information. We want you to be able to deal with anger in a way that does not jeopardize the value and safety of your relationship.

Before examining the relationship between anger and trauma in more depth, let's consider the experience of Hal and Marsha:

Hal and Marsha were struggling to survive the death of their nineteen-year-old son from a drug overdose. Both had barely managed the first six months after his death by just going through the motions of living. Now it seemed to Hal that either they were arguing all the time or the house was completely silent. Everything and anything could lead to an argument, and they were both likely to lash out and say things they would later regret. Both had some awareness that they were angry about losing John, but neither had any idea how to interrupt the negative spiral they were caught in.

Their relationship had always been a little volatile—they had often fought about trivial things, but they had always managed to kiss and make up without looking back. Those fights rarely led to the kind of personal lashing-out that was occurring now. They needed to understand and learn to control this destructive fighting before they did greater damage to their relationship.

At the suggestion of a fellow teacher and close friend, Marsha began to read some booklets about traumatic loss of a loved one. She shared these with Hal. Together, they read about trauma and anger and began to understand how, when we are stressed, negative feelings of any kind often trip associations with angry feelings and actions. Just having this little bit of information began to shift things at home. While they still could not talk calmly together about their unimaginable loss, at least they were on the same side as they tried to reduce their painful reactions to it.

More and more they became like a research team, looking online, finding articles, and giving them to one another to read. Eventually, they were able to read more about what had happened—they began to look at substance abuse and drug-related deaths. They still argued, but learning more about their son's death reduced the tension and anger somewhat. The time they had spent trying to understand the tragedy had actually given them shared nonreactive time and, drawing upon that experience, they agreed to set some ground rules and boundaries around expressing anger. They agreed that either of them could announce, "We are over the line" and that they would then tone it down or stop until they could talk about the issue more calmly.

This brief glimpse at Marsha and Hal's experience illustrates that reactions to traumatic events often become a secondary source of trauma, and anger is one such reaction. We see, however, that when people act upon their urge to make meaning of the event, they begin to take back control of their negative reactions. Like Marsha and Hal, when partners can do this together, they find a light at the end of the tunnel. This chapter is intended to help you find that light.

Taking the Historical Pulse of Your Anger

Stephen Mitchell (2002, 120) wisely said, "The survival of romance depends not on skill in avoiding aggression but on the capacity to contain it alongside love." In approaching the issue of how and why anger is a part of trauma, we need to first understand that anger plays a part in any relationship. Therefore, to understand how the trauma you have experienced is related to the anger you or your partner may be feeling, you'll want to think about how you and your partner experienced and handled anger in your relationship prior to these recent events.

You quite likely followed established patterns of repair and recovery for dealing with anger. Perhaps your relationship was stormy, with many highs and lows and frequent expressions of anger, or maybe it was quiet and calm, with angry feelings held in check and expressed only with great difficulty and control. Some relationships are a mix of two very different partners—one who may be too quick to express anger and another who silently seethes.

In the aftermath of trauma, patterns rarely shift in a radical way. More commonly they become more exaggerated. For example, those whose past tendency had been to withdraw when angry are likely to withdraw even more in the face of anger escalated by stress. Those with a quick temper and a history of flying off the handle may seem even more reactive and aggressive. Occasionally, however, the partner with a long history of holding back anger may, in the aftermath of trauma, no longer be able to do so. Angry outbursts from this partner may seem so out of character that they are more frightening and disturbing than the same level of expression from someone who typically expresses their anger.

Ask yourselves the following questions about how you handled anger in the past:

* Did you feel that you had permission to feel angry in your relationship?

* How was anger expressed?

* Was anger the dominant feeling in the relationship?

* Did you argue over only the big issues, or were trivial things often the trigger?

- Did you have similar or different ways of dealing with anger?

- Did you take turns regulating each other's moods?

- Was one of you the agitator and one the soother?

- Could you calm each other down in anger-provoking situations?

- Was the expression of anger different early in your relationship?

- Did you learn over time to handle it more comfortably?

- Over time, did you lose track of how to forgive or forget?

- Were you able to argue without the argument becoming a fight?

- Did one or both of you know how to let it go?

- Did your arguments or fights lead to constructive decisions?

- Did the fights simply become destructive verbal attacks?

- Did the fights become physically dangerous?

- Did you have a way to recover?

It is quite possible that you have never given much thought to these issues. Some partners are aware of how each deals with anger and how to live with the ups and downs without much reflection or discussion: perhaps he would wait for her to calm down before approaching, or she learned to apologize or tease him back into a good mood, or both would just wait for it to blow over. Some partners just ride out rocky times; others keep trying to get it right. Some start giving up. Whatever the historical pulse of anger in your relationship, your goal now is to minimize or change what did not work in handling anger and maximize and expand coping strategies that worked well.

The Relationship Between Trauma and Anger

Findings show that in trauma-exposed adults anger and hostility are associated with post-traumatic stress disorder (PTSD) in the aftermath of all types of traumatic events (Orth and Wieland 2006). Anger is a common and complex response to trauma even for those who do not develop PTSD, because anger can be experienced as a physiological state, an emotion, a way of thinking, a behavioral response, or a combination of these.

Anger as a Physical Response

Anger often accompanies trauma because it is basic to the fight-or-flight reaction to threat or danger. In situations of danger our biological arousal system causes an increase in heart rate; rapid, shallow breathing; cold sweats; tingling muscular tension; and at times antagonistic behavior (Levine 1997; van der Kolk, McFarlane, and Weisaeth 1996). These physiological reactions peak and then should diminish; however, in the aftermath of trauma, the body often continues to react as if it were still facing the threat of annihilation. People find themselves reacting with intense negative emotions, like fear, anxiety, anger, and panic, to what others would consider rather neutral or mildly distressing stimuli. The autonomic nervous system, which has the important function of alerting us to potential danger, is no longer functioning properly. Our threshold for reactivity has changed—now a traffic jam becomes cause for rage, or a partner's locking the keys in the car becomes the trigger for verbal aggression.

Anger as a Mask of Other Feelings

Another theory explaining the relationship between anger and traumatic stress is the fear avoidance theory (Feeny, Zoellner, and Foa 2000). It suggests that anger may be used to avoid feelings of fear caused by the memories, nightmares, flashbacks, and other intrusions of trauma. It's possible that you or your partner may prefer to be angry at the thought of what happened than to reexperience the fear felt at the time.

Anger is often a secondary response used to defend against feelings of vulnerability, helplessness, and shame (the urge to hide in order to avoid being seen as different from the way you want to be seen). In the aftermath of trauma people are often aware of their vulnerability, high level of anxiety, sense of loss, and need for others. This awareness creates shame because such feelings are so different from the person's usual view of him- or herself. Most people need to consciously and unconsciously hide feelings of shame from themselves as well as the rest of the world. They prefer to see the world as dangerous or hostile and react with vigilance and anger than feel the shame associated with feeling frightened, vulnerable, or bereft (Lansky 2000).

Consistent with this, the rage that many military personnel, police officers, and firefighters experience when injured and removed from duty illustrates how injury clashes with their necessary view of themselves as invulnerable. When they hold on to this rage and it spills over to their partners, it becomes self-destructive and destructive of their relationships.

The Relationship Between Anger and Depression

Increasing evidence shows that depression is a common sequel to the experience of trauma. Depression is often related to grief over the traumatic loss of the known self, the loss of another person, and the loss of our assumptions that we are worthwhile and safe and that the world is just and meaningful (Janoff-Bulman 1989). We know that depression is often experienced after disasters and is the most common disorder suffered in conjunction with post-traumatic stress disorder (Ursano, Grieger, and McCarroll 1996). It is helpful to recognize that in men depression is more likely to be expressed in an increase in fatigue, irritability, and anger (National Institute of Mental Health 2005). So the anger felt and expressed by men after a traumatic event may actually be a sign of depression.

The connection between depression and anger has been found in a number of studies with veterans. These studies reveal that when veterans are suffering with depression as well as PTSD they are at greater risk for domestic violence (Taft et al. 2005; 2007). One explanation is that feelings of anxiety and depression (often called *dysphoric* symptoms) may lower inhibitions that would ordinarily limit aggressiveness; the depressed person may feel that nothing, including controlling one's anger or aggressive behavior, really matters (Chemtob et al. 1997). Such aggression often has a reckless, self-destructive aspect that reflects the underlying feelings of despair and hopelessness.

Another explanation for the connection between trauma, depression, and anger is a person's recognition of his or her loss of resources (Hobfoll 1989). This theory suggests that a person first registers the traumatic loss, injury, or illness, and then with time (for example, being home for six months with a combat injury, or being unable to rebuild the family home or find employment after a natural disaster) he or she becomes aware of the loss of potential, ability, vitality, health, earnings, and so on. This awareness can trigger a loss of self-esteem and autonomy. The anger that results is a stress reaction. This cycle may explain the anger and relationship problems that often emerge a number of months after a disaster or redeployment (Lane and Hobfoll 1992).

Anger in First Responders and Members of the Military

Both the meaning of trauma and the experience of anger are different for first responders, those in the military, and their partners. Because of self-selection, training, and the nature of their missions, these groups have a different threshold for trauma than most civilians have. They expect to face life-threatening situations that would ordinarily engender fear, helplessness, and horror. Survival and success warrant that they stay dissociated from feelings, maintain a level of hyperarousal and tactical awareness, and remain focused on their mission. Police and military personnel are trained to harness and use targeted aggression to secure the safety of others and protect their own—they need to be vigilant, forceful, and quick to act. This command presence and battle-mind mentality is very difficult for police and military personnel to put down at home and with family members, and often factors into angry disruptions.

Those who have worked with military and first responders suggest that, although their threshold for trauma may be higher, they never become immune to the horror and death that they continually face (Rudofossi 2007; Henry 2004). In order to function in their jobs, they may often use anger to avoid experiencing and reacting to feelings like sadness or loss. Nonetheless, these feelings are there. It is often the mission in which a buddy is killed or a child dies that tips the scale from anger to traumatic stress symptoms. Soothing by a spouse or partner that might reduce anger or anguish is often sabotaged by the code of silence in these cultures and the expectation of not being understood. For example, consider the impact of anger on the relationship of Phil and Kathy.

In the aftermath of 9/11, Phil's rage at the loss of his brother as well as his fire-department comrades kept him anesthetized. In those first months working at Ground Zero, he could feel neither his loss nor the attempts by his wife and children to be there for him. Frozen in his rage, Phil was determined never to forget. As is often the case for first responders, when the mission was over and Ground Zero was closed, it became increasingly difficult for Phil to wall himself off from his grief and he began drinking heavily. With her support efforts rebuffed, and finding it almost impossible to be a compassionate presence to someone whose anger and irritability were fueled by alcohol, Kathy wrote Phil a letter explaining that she could not continue without changes being made to his drinking and in their relationship. Reading the note, Phil was hit with the reality that he could lose her—she would leave. Not knowing what to say, he just started writing back. It was the start of their recovery. In an unexpected way, notes and e-mail sent back and forth between them became the trail back to each other. Once Phil started addressing his drinking, he could write and eventually talk about the anger without being angry at Kathy and the world. They started sharing the pain of losing loved ones and eventually the special memories they held for them. Sometimes the notes were only a line or two. Sometimes the notes referred to a memory; other times they mentioned something that bothered one about the other. Occasionally the notes prompted a discussion. Slowly they found a way to recapture what they had lost as a couple.

The "written exchange" strategy that Phil and Kathy spontaneously used will be discussed at the end of this chapter. It fits with what Lieutenant Colonel Dave Grossman (2004, 262) tells us about recovery from grief, "Pain shared is pain divided."

Understanding How and Why Anger Erupts

Very often, couples who have faced trauma report, "We never fought this much before. Why now?" There are a number of reasons why anger may erupt between partners in the aftermath of trauma: changes in needs, denial of feelings, need to blame, displacement of feelings, projection of feelings, and miscommunication.

Changes in Needs

Trauma assaults us on physical, emotional, social, and cognitive levels. After trauma, even the needs of the most resilient couples are greater. People need more physical help or emotional support from their partner just to keep going. Adjusting to the myriad of changes they have faced can be exhausting, and because they may feel more helpless and vulnerable, they often need their partner to agree with them more or mirror the feelings they are having. However, it's rare for people to realize this about themselves. Rather, they have less tolerance for differences of opinion, mistakes, or oversights. Feeling more insecure, they may interpret their partner's actions in a negative way and then retaliate in a negative way—setting the stage for the fight they don't understand! Unfortunately, the real cause stays hidden, the impact of trauma on them is overlooked, and they keep repeating the same type of fight. Let's see how this plays out in the example of Sue and Carl:

*Sue and Carl reported that they really loved each other and
had held together as a team after she was diagnosed with breast
cancer, had surgery, and went through chemotherapy. During
the month of recuperation that followed, Sue cut back at work,
and Carl stepped up and took more responsibility for the house.
Somehow through it all, meals were cooked, the house was
cleaned, and bills got paid. The problem was that they were often
at each other's throats. In the past, before the cancer, if she had
asked him to pick up milk and he forgot, she might have teased
him a little and one of them would have gone to get it, or they
would have let it go. Now, forgetting the milk was another reason
for going at it:*

Sue: Did you get the milk?

Carl: No, I forgot it.

Sue: Is there anything you can remember?

Carl: Here we go. That's right, I can't do anything right. Maybe
         it's time for you to get it yourself.

Sue: Do you think I like depending on you?

Sue: [Carl walks into another room. Sue follows him.] Please
         don't walk away from me.

Carl: [Refuses to answer.]

Sue: [Crying] So now you are not going to speak to me.

Carl: [Turns on the TV.]

Sue: I need to talk to you.

Carl: No, you need to put me down.

The exchange between Sue and Carl illustrates a typical way in
which anger erupts between couples in the aftermath of trauma. It is
common for couples to handle the crisis time well, only to fall apart once
the worst is over. Sue and Carl's fight was not about the milk or Carl's
memory, but rather the accumulated feelings that accompanied the shift

in roles and responsibilities—a shift that had changed the balance in their relationship. Carl was feeling unappreciated for his efforts to keep it all going and was longing for the return of his strong and capable wife. Sue hated finding herself so dependent on Carl but was unable to express this directly. Despite their effective functioning during the crisis, they were still unable to really talk about the fears it stirred up, the changes it created, and how they would work to create a new balance.

Denial of Feelings

Like Sue and Carl, some couples can't speak about the fear or loss associated with the trauma. Although they have faced it together, it is as if *putting words to it* makes it too real. Sometimes there is an unspoken collusion to keep the fear and loss out of the partners' consciousness. Neither Sue nor Carl dealt with the loss of her healthy, independent self. Even as she regained her strength and most of her independence, they were still unable to celebrate because of the unspoken fear of a recurrence. In a sense, they did not give themselves an opportunity to mourn the loss of who they were before the cancer. Nor did they use their successful teamwork to affirm their resilience and redefine themselves as a strong couple. As a result, the only expression of feelings became the anger that erupted between them.

Need to Blame

Given that traumatic events are unexpected assaults on our sense of mortality, predictability, safety, and control, it is natural for people to need to reestablish the illusion of control. In other words, it seems that someone has to be blamed. If someone or something can be blamed, then perhaps the pain and the loss were preventable. Notwithstanding those cases where the traumatic event is the direct result of another human's malicious intent to harm, there is often a tendency to blame the victim—even by the victim him- or herself. There can be unspoken blame for getting shot, being in the accident, not preparing for the tornado, or even getting sick, which is manifested in the form of anger and fighting between the partners. Sometimes it is disguised as blame for minor things. Alternatively, blame can also be clearly stated: "Why did you go out so late?" "I asked you not to reenlist." "Who takes his eyes off a three-year-old on a jungle gym?"

Far from reinstating the feeling of safety and control, blame of a partner only leads to pain. When people have done something to hurt themselves or someone else, they know it. If they have endured trauma because of someone or some event, they rarely need to be reminded of it.

> *It had been eight months since John's car accident and there was quite a bit of tension and anger between John and his wife, Carla. For her part, Carla did not understand why John was mad at her instead of at the driver who had cost him his vision in one eye. What John was actually angry about, but did not explain, was Carla's continual tirades against the driver, which reminded him of the accident and his physical disability.*

When blame is directed at a partner, either for causing the traumatic event or for bringing up uncomfortable feelings, it only serves to fuel more anger. Often blame sets off shame, which is then covered by rage as a way of avoiding self-hate and self-loathing.

Need to Regulate Feelings

As we discussed in chapter 2, the bond between most couples is so strong that the physical presence of the partner or even a phone conversation with him or her can regulate mood, feelings, and bodily states. For example, before she left for Iraq, all Jean had to do was see Danny walk into a room to feel love and connection. Similarly, even an e-mail from her could brighten his mood. It is this conscious and unconscious bond, this appropriate "use" of the other that often becomes misused in the aftermath of trauma. Sometimes after trauma people will displace their anger toward others onto their safe person, the person who loves them— their partner. Other times, they may project their own anger or negative feelings onto their partner, accusing their partner of having those very feelings. Let's look at these two concepts a little more closely:

Displacement

When feelings of anger cannot be directed toward their source, they may consciously or often unconsciously be displaced onto the partner. Frequently this is accomplished by provoking the partner into a fight. We can observe this with Jean and Danny on her return from Iraq.

Struggling with sleep disturbance and physical symptoms, Jean was miserable returning full-time to nursing. Angry at the loss of comrades, unable to relax, and feeling "out of it," she would often come home complaining about someone or something and insist that Danny think or feel the same way. His refusal to immediately agree with her would trip her anger toward him. Being accused of lack of support and caring, Danny would become defensive, and the fight would begin.

Projection

Another underlying dynamic that involves misusing a partner to regulate feelings is called *projective identification*. This means that if a person is unable to recognize a negative feeling like anger, despair, mistrust, or jealousy as his or her own, then that person may unconsciously project the feeling onto the partner and then criticize or attack the partner for having this feeling.

Jean would continually accuse Danny of not loving her as much as he had before Iraq and insist that he believed they could no longer be happy. These feelings were really a projection of Jean's own fears and doubts. Such projections incited rage in Danny, who felt misjudged and attacked. The fights resulted in a confusing and vicious cycle with neither knowing how the other really felt.

Anger as Miscommunication

We have underscored that having a relationship from which to draw strength and support is a valuable resource in the aftermath of trauma. Part and parcel of a supportive relationship is the understanding between partners of the need for differences, space, time, and privacy. Given the common urge to care for or to be cared for by the other after trauma, the communication of such needs is often difficult. Suppressed by some, silenced by others, it often does not happen clearly. Anger, whether conscious or unconscious, becomes the method of communicating the need for space, time alone, and the like. It may become the way to avoid expected or unwanted intimacy or the means to regulate distance. At times it is the unconscious way of refusing to revisit the trauma their partner wants to talk about.

Unfortunately, this seldom works, because the message it sends cannot be understood by the partner. The partner does not know that the anger is actually about avoiding intimacy or just needing to be alone. By fighting rather than talking, the partners have no chance of understanding, for example, that they each might need to revisit the memory, thoughts, and feelings associated with trauma at different times and in different ways.

> *Paul's late-night complaints to Carol about money or projects around the house were really a way to avoid Carol's wish to talk about losing the baby or the possibility of sexual connection, which could lead to another pregnancy—neither of which he could handle. Experienced by Carol as hostility and rejection, these complaints often erupted into fighting and ended up with distance between them.*

The Importance of Expressing Anger

Couples recovering from trauma often ask if anger can be damaging in the aftermath of trauma. The basic answer is no. Anger is a human feeling and in itself is not damaging. However, what you do with it and what it does to you can be. It is *impossible* for partners in a relationship to never feel anger. In fact, one of the problem reactions of some couples in the aftermath of trauma is the fear of and avoidance of anger—the walking on eggshells. Often we hear things like "I don't want to bring up anything to upset him," "I don't want to rock the boat," and "It is better that I just keep my mouth closed."

We believe that if it is not safe to fight in a relationship, then it is not a safe relationship. In addition, if each partner can't be authentic with feelings, then spontaneity and real connection are not possible. Not only are there some fights worth having; there are also constructive ways to disagree, to express anger, and even to fight that move a relationship forward, keep it alive, and validate its resiliency.

Before we consider how to handle anger in a constructive way, let's look more closely at why and how anger between partners becomes destructive to them and the bond they share.

The Path from Trauma to Destructive Anger

The path from trauma to destructive anger can be tragic and dangerous. It includes behaviors that fuel the fight, and lead to destructive consequences like frozen resentment, verbal abuse, or physical violence. In our work we have found that, once anger has been stirred in one or both of the partners, it can erupt into a fight because, often without realizing it, partners fuel the fight.

Behaviors That Fuel the Fight

Behaviors that fuel the fight are listed below. By identifying and understanding them, you can give yourselves an opportunity to reconsider the impact of some of your behaviors and reduce the likelihood of fighting:

- **Taking anger personally.** Interpreting your partner's irritability or anger as a personal attack to which you must react.

- **Inability to observe yourself.** Being unable to step back to consider the cause of your own anger, your overreactivity, or your provocation of your partner's anger.

- **Inability to see the broader context.** Being unable to see the offense, disagreement, or oversight in the context of what is going on in each of your lives. When you can't see the broader context, you can't ask whether this is a fight worth having.

- **Not giving yourself permission for time and space.** The inability to take time out to calm down and rethink the situation deprives you of the ability to move from an emotionally driven "me-versus-you" survival mentality to a place where rational thinking, problem solving, or empathy can take place. In refusing to let your partner step away to calm down, save face, or self-observe, you actually fuel irrational and aggressive behavior and lock out reasoning or resolution.

- **Ignoring the circumstances.** You may have a strong desire to talk about the issue or problem right away. However, when you choose to begin a discussion without considering the current circumstances, you let your urgency to deal with the issue jeopardize the possibility of a better outcome. For example, you probably won't have the best results if you argue when your partner is tired, hungry, drunk, or upset about something else. Similarly, bringing up an argument in front of family, friends, or children adds factors like shame, embarrassment, or guilt to the situation, which usually escalates the fighting.

- **Being verbally aggressive.** When you attack your partner with taunts, personal insults, accusations, and threats of separation or divorce, he or she feels assaulted and may retaliate or withdraw. Such verbal attacks are remembered and decay the trust or affirmation necessary for genuine intimacy.

- **Using silence as punishment.** The "silent treatment" is both provocative and assaultive. Refusing to talk despite the other's attempts to apologize or positively reconnect is actually an in-your-face statement that you are withholding connection, respect, and the opportunity to resolve the problem.

- **Creating shame.** Assaulting a partner's sense of value or worth by criticizing personal habits, traits, or behaviors or reminding the partner of mistakes or insecurities is dangerous as it generally provokes primitive rage.

- **Use of alcohol or drugs.** Using alcohol or drugs before or during an angry exchange is like pouring lighter fluid on a small flame. It eliminates the possibility of bringing a rational perspective to the situation and increases negative feelings.

Exercise: Recognizing Behaviors That Fuel the Fight

Read the following list of behaviors and put a check mark next to any behaviors that apply to you and your partner. Note that you may have an easier time identifying your partner's behaviors than your own. Read them alone, take turns reading them, or perhaps read them together, openly considering what behaviors fuel the fights between you. Use the space provided to write any notes that might be helpful to you.

Behavior	You	Partner
Taking anger personally	_____	_____
Inability to self-observe	_____	_____
Inability to see the broader context	_____	_____
Not giving permission for time and space	_____	_____
Ignoring the circumstances	_____	_____
Being verbally aggressive	_____	_____
Using silence as punishment	_____	_____
Creating shame	_____	_____
Using alcohol or drugs	_____	_____

Destructive Consequences

Once the anger moves into fight mode, the consequences are most often destructive. They may include the following:

- **Verbal aggression.** Verbal assaults and degrading comments not only destroy the fabric of trust, safety, and intimacy in a relationship, but they can also provoke physical aggression. Studies of intimate partner violence find that verbal aggression is a predictor of physical aggression and marital decline (Schumacher and Leonard 2005).

- **Emotional abuse.** Continual fighting, accusing, criticism, and so on takes a toll on both partners. Such fighting robs each of a partner, since it often destroys the self-esteem of the abused partner and leaves the other unhappy, guilty, and emotionally alone.

- **Physical violence.** Once the line has been crossed, and physical violence has occurred between partners, the situation is dangerous. We know that one incident greatly increases the probability of another. In that case, it is time for both to seek help in order to ensure their safety. If the violence is ignored, the situation will not improve.

- **Atmosphere of fear.** When partners live in the shadow of verbal or physical violence, authentic feelings have stopped being possible. In many cases, one or the other leaves, physically or psychologically, sometimes using a substance as a means of escape.

- **Physical debilitation from symptoms of chronic stress.** An often hidden but serious consequence of destructive fighting and anger between partners is physical decline and illness. Due to the connection between mind and body, ongoing fighting between partners often results in chronic stress, which greatly compromises the body's immune system.

- **Breakup and divorce.** Whether a result of cycles of destructive fighting or resentment, many relationships and marriages fail in an atmosphere of destructive anger.

Given these destructive consequences, it is vitally important that you put strategies in place to alter the path from trauma to destructive anger. In most cases, the earlier the intervention, the easier the path and the better the outcome. If you recognize that you have a great deal of destructive anger and fighting in your relationship, consider using the anger management strategies listed in the next section and the guidelines for making an anger management plan. If along the way you decide to seek professional help to deal with anger and management issues between you, you may be making one of the most important decisions of your relationship. It has been our experience that it is *never too late* to fight for your relationship!

Anger Management for Couples

Researchers have found that there are three components to thriving in the face of adversity that may help a couple deal with anger and negative feelings in the aftermath of trauma: commitment, control, and challenge (Maddi 2002). We believe that anger can be managed effectively within a relationship if partners have a *mutual commitment* to respect and protect each other from destructive anger, use preventive steps and communication to control the escalation of anger, and take on the challenge of couple anger management. Let's take a closer look at ways of preventing destructive anger, communicating effectively, and developing a couple anger management plan.

Preventing Destructive Anger

Perhaps the most crucial means for preventing destructive anger is to understand the reasons for your anger. You can start by thinking about what you have learned in this chapter about fueling and expressing destructive anger. It has been shown that awareness produced by thinking and learning about anger actually alters angry, harsh, or impulsive behavior (Berkowitz 1990). If you and your partner work on understanding and thinking about anger, you will likely be better prepared to respond in constructive ways.

You may recall the principles of couples psychological first aid, which we discussed in chapter 2. A number of the strategies described there involve partner care and are particularly valuable in preventing anger. Let's look at how these principles can be used to help prevent anger:

Making the Relationship Safe for Feelings

Anger often masks other feelings. If you and your partner feel safe enough in your relationship so that either of you can feel sad, disappointed, frightened, tired, jealous, lonely, and so on without repercussions—if you can be compassionate toward each other in the face of feelings—there will be less need to mask feelings with anger.

Physical Care

As we've discussed, there is a physiological component to anger in the aftermath of trauma, due to the fight-or-flight response as well as hyperarousal, intrusion, and constriction symptoms. These have an impact on sleep, hypersensitivity to stimuli, numbing, and avoidance of feelings. Physical care of oneself and one's partner—providing gentle support and encouragement to reset the body's sleeping, eating, and relaxing rhythms—goes a long way in preventing anger.

Connection with Other Social and Emotional Supports

Connecting with outside friends and activities to lower stress, share feelings, and exchange ideas is valuable for both of you. Spouses of military personnel often receive very beneficial support from being with others who understand the challenges of readjusting after redeployment. Spending time with other family members and friends can also add to the feeling of being supported and replenished.

However, when people attempt to use friends, colleagues, or relatives to help solve their marital problems or complain about their partner, then this resource is being misused. Overdisclosure of personal issues is rarely helpful and, more importantly, creates issues of trust in the relationship and strain in the connection between your partner and the friends or relatives involved. If you find that you are beginning to engage with others in this way, it may be a signal that you need to talk to a professional.

Using Effective Communication

Couples can use language to make war, or to make love—in other words, to prevent destructive anger and fighting and increase their positive communication. Fostering effective communication involves two components: speaking in a way that allows your partner to listen, and listening in a way that encourages the partner to speak.

Speaking So That Your Partner Can Listen

If you are angry with your partner, you may have the urge to send a negative you-message in the form of criticism, blame, put-downs, accusations, or even threats. For example, you might say things like "How can you be so stupid?" "You are the reason the kids are so upset," "Why must you ruin every dinner?" or "You make it so difficult to be with you."

These messages are ineffective—they never resolve anything. Instead they simply fuel the fight. Although you might feel you are venting some anger and clearing the air, you are actually adding to the problem. At the very least, your partner is not likely to understand the reason for your anger because most partners stop listening as soon as the tone gets critical or blameful. Any real discussion of the reason for your anger becomes impossible, and the stage is set for resentment, misunderstanding, more verbal aggression, and even physical aggression.

In the discussion on couples psychological first aid in chapter 2 we introduced the idea of sending an I-message rather than a you-message when you are trying to improve communication with your partner. Let's utilize them here. Try replacing negative you-messages with I-messages that describe how you feel. For example, if Mary says to Richard, "I don't think I can manage all the chores by myself—I'm simply exhausted," this sends a message that is different from "You do nothing around here and I'm sick of it!" By describing her feelings with an I-message, Mary has provided information that clarifies how she feels and what she needs.

Often, when we are sharing this technique with couples, a partner will say, "What do you mean, what do I feel? I feel angry." We ask these partners to consider what other feelings they are having. Sometimes a closer look reveals the feeling preceding or associated with the anger. Here are a couple of scenarios and their related I- and you-messages:

Your partner is late coming home and doesn't call.

Negative you-message: When your partner finally comes home, you say, "You just don't care. Why didn't you call?"

More effective I-message: When your partner finally comes home, you say, "I was frightened that something had happened to you. It would help me to know if you are going to be late."

Your partner keeps criticizing you in front of her friends and family.

Negative you-message: You say, "If you keep acting like a bitch in front of your friends and family, I'm out of here."

More effective I-message: You say, "I feel embarrassed when you put me down in front of other people."

Listening in a Way That Encourages Your Partner to Speak

Let's go back to Mary and Richard. When Mary says, "I don't think I can manage all the chores by myself—I'm simply exhausted," if Richard ignores her, walks out of the room, tells her to pay for more help, or makes a sarcastic remark, then it is likely she will react with resentment, become more angry, or verbally retaliate with increasing anger. When this happens, nothing can be resolved. Richard will have missed a chance to understand how she feels as well as to share his reaction and feelings.

Active listening. If Richard were to use active listening skills (described in chapter 2), he would listen, try to put himself in Mary's shoes, and then let her know what he had heard her say. For example, he might say, "Wow, I guess you really have too much on your plate right now," or "You sound overloaded right now; I'm feeling the same way." While each response is quite different, both let her know he has heard her and offer a chance to talk rather than fight about it.

Fear of active listening. In our work with couples, one of the things we have found is that partners are often afraid of listening. Worried about each other and stressed themselves, partners fear hearing that their partner is upset. They fear that if there is a problem they must solve it, they fear being blamed, and they fear having to endure more change. We encourage them to consider that active listening is itself a solution to the fear and stress of trauma. (See chapter 2 for more detailed discussion of active listening.)

In those cases where a partner has a problem that involves the other partner, effective communication in the form of I-messages and active listening is not only a preventive aggression strategy—it also lays the groundwork for joint problem solving and conflict resolution, which we will discuss later in this chapter.

Developing a Couple Anger Management Plan

Given that we are human, it is likely that, even with superb efforts at prevention, angry feelings will sometimes spark a fight. As stated earlier, this in and of itself is quite normal, and you may feel that you manage these situations well. However, if you or your partner is having trouble dealing with anger and outbursts are escalating, we strongly suggest that you develop and use a couple anger management plan.

When you are developing a plan, we suggest breaking things down into three more-manageable tasks: defusing anger, fair fighting, and resolution. Next you will find strategies for these three tasks.

Defusing Anger

The following approaches can be used to minimize the amount and intensity of anger in your relationship. While they can be developed and practiced by each of you independently, the more you communicate about them together, the more success you are likely to have.

Self-observation and regulation. Stepping back to observe yourself even for a few moments may give you time and perspective to better understand your feelings of anger. Are they originating in you? Are they a function of fatigue, pain, or fear? If so, consider sharing that understanding with your partner. For example, you might say, "You know what? I think I'm just cranky from not sleeping."

Each of you may also need your own plan to regulate your angry feelings. Think about what you do that helps you calm down. For some people it may be physical activity like walking, jogging, or even cleaning. Others calm down listening to music, surfing the Web, or doing crosswords. Using such techniques can help you to step back from the fight and return later, when you are calmer and better able to discuss your needs or issues. Once you are aware of what you use to calm yourself, let your partner know. This will help both of you support each other's coping strategies.

Stepping on the brakes together. Learn to step back and ask, "Why are we fighting about this? There has to be another way to deal with this problem." Doing this individually or together on a regular basis during minor disagreements will increase the likelihood of your stepping on the brakes again when it is needed during more serious arguments. Sometimes humor is a wonderful way to step on the brakes and defuse the fight: "Wait a minute—we're turning into my parents! Nothing is worth that."

Cognitive restructuring. Thinking about the circumstances along with the actions or behavior of your partner may put it into another perspective. Is it conceivable that the situation you are angry about may have a different meaning? Could it have been a miscommunication, a misunderstanding, or an accident? How you think about it will affect how you feel about it and how you react to it.

Letting go. Once you are done with a disagreement, let it go. You may think that telling your partner what you *were* angry about is part of letting go. It is not. Rarely will your partner be grateful for such information. In fact, it usually dampens the mood, creates stress, or actually triggers a fight. Also, take care not to use it as ammunition in a fight later on—this would only cause mistrust and stress.

Outing the inner dialogue. Think about the things you are saying to yourself but have not said out loud. When you have figured out what you are actually angry about, practice saying it, not in an angry way but in a manner that is communicative and informational. For example, don't fight about cereal brands if you are really uncomfortable about his being home since his injury and his habit of constantly checking on you and asking you what you are doing. Discussing your feelings about this situation might lead you both to consider the impact of your new and changed roles.

Finding new ways to communicate. Sometimes a couple needs to find their own creative way to communicate. If you just can't seem to talk because you are feeling too much pain, shame, or resentment, experiment with the "written exchange." This can be done by e-mail, in a notebook that you share, or in notes that you leave in a certain predictable place. Write about how you feel. If you are using a notebook to write notes back and forth, write the time, date, and your entry in a spot where your partner can read it and write his or her response below (also marked with the time and date). Essentially these notes are a way of saying, "I want to stay connected; I want to communicate." Taken seriously, the written note can be a very valuable way to defuse anger, build trust, and provide the opportunity for more understanding.

Of course, the written word is not for everyone. For some, a daily ten-minute coffee break that you spend together can allow you to communicate volumes. You might choose some early-morning time when you can steal a few minutes to share a thought before the day takes off. The catch-up phone call during the commute home or after you drop the kids at school can also become a predictable, welcomed connection. You may find that using that time to take turns sharing a feeling, memory, or experience while your partner just listens can be quite soothing; what's important is not the words but rather the sharing. Some prefer just finding a time to be together—holding hands, taking a walk, or making eye contact—to communicate commitment during difficult times.

Fair Fighting

Sometimes it happens: despite attempts to defuse the anger or discord, a fight erupts. In such a situation, it is crucial that as a couple you know that you are both safe—that you can be enraged and still care for and love each other. To guarantee fair fighting, consider using the following strategies:

Establish safety. Agree to never harm the other physically or verbally. Any sign of potential physical violence needs to be taken seriously and warrants help and support for you both. If you feel you are in a situation where safety boundaries are unclear, when things calm down let your partner know that you would like to have a serious conversation. Approach this issue as calmly as you would any other serious relationship issue, such as planning a family, writing your will, or considering relocation. When you sit down to have the conversation, consider working together to clearly define the line that neither of you will ever physically or verbally cross. Certainly any physical contact made in anger is unacceptable and warrants a quick and safe exit plan to protect both of you. Make suggestions so that you have a plan to leave the room, house, or situation if needed. Recognize together that outside help may be needed. Because verbal aggression is often the preface to physical aggression, it is important to also protect each other from saying the unsayable—insults, hurtful name calling, or provocation of the other. Come up with some suggestions and a basic agreement about safe talking—for example, "When we have a disagreement, we will talk for a set amount of time, we will write down the problem, we will take turns giving our opinion, we can take a few days to solve it, and we will not talk when one of us is tired, hungry, or drinking." If there are certain ways you would not want your children or parents treated or spoken to, and then agree not to treat or speak to each other in that way.

Disengagement and reengagement. Respect each other's need for space and time even in an argument. If one partner says he or she can't deal with the issue anymore, then both of you have to hit the pause button and return to the issue at a later time. This pause is actually a safety valve for both. Too often, the partner who wants to keep talking gets anxious, assumes nothing will be resolved, and ignores the request by either pushing more or closing down in an angry way. If, instead, a partner can actually allow the disengagement, knowing the other partner will agree to talk about it at another time, it becomes possible to discuss the issue with less reactivity. In the process, both of you will have the experience of trusting each other and mutually regulating your anger in discussions, a useful skill that you will be able to use again in the future.

Own your projections and feelings. Whenever you presume to know what your partner thinks or feels and you accuse him or her based on that presumption, stop the tape. People often feel enraged when they are being told what they feel, and presumptions about another person keep hostility going because they result in a closed and static system. There is no open space for understanding. For example, if you assume your partner is rejecting you and you retaliate with anger and criticism, you are in a closed system that doesn't allow in your partner's true feelings.

Whenever you realize that you have told your partner what he or she thinks or feels, take a step back and consider saying, "I'm sorry, I'm assuming I know what you are thinking, and I don't. Can you tell me what's going on with you?"

In addition, if you are open to self-reflection, you may realize that the feelings you have attached to your partner actually belong to you. If this is the case, try owning those feelings: "You know, maybe it's me who is afraid of things changing, not you," or "I guess I figure that you must be in a bad mood, because that's how I'm feeling." This kind of self-awareness not only leads to healing and growth for you as an individual, but can also create safety and newfound openness in your partner.

Finding Resolution. The word "resolution" can refer to a decision to do something (like a New Year's resolution), or an outcome or solution to a problem. In a way, when partners come to a resolution, both meanings apply. Their decision to do something together to prevent, defuse, or change the anger in their relationship is a crucial step in recovery. The actual resolution they come to may make a major difference in their lives and reflect their commitment and trust. This is true even if it is only a working resolution, one that suggests, "At the moment this works but we will keep talking and amending it as the journey of recovery unfolds." *Agreeing to disagree for the time being, accepting that you are both trying to be patient with the other, realizing that if you use your resilience as a couple a plan will emerge—this is a working resolution.*

Time has a way of putting things in perspective, which fosters resolution. The anxiety and anger about a certain issue often looks and feels very different when it is revisited the next morning or in a few days, weeks, or months. Life is not a sitcom—recovery is a process, not a quick fix.

Prioritizing the relationship. Being clear about your priorities as a couple can help you move beyond disagreements or fighting in order to come to some resolution. It is likely that you prioritize various factors when quickly working out small differences, like what movie to see or food to eat. At such times you are probably often putting the happiness of your partner and the feeling between you ahead of your choice of movie or restaurant. Similarly, if you begin to ask, "Is this the fight worth having?" you are choosing harmony and connection over the issue itself. If you continually find yourselves in power struggles without the ability to give and take, ask yourself, "Do I want to win or do I want to be together?" The type of prioritizing required in a relationship is different from prioritizing your workload or a list of home improvements. Again, you are really making the relationship between you, or at times your partner's need, the highest priority.

Handling value clashes. When the issue that erupts into a fight or argument is actually a value clash of greater significance, finding a resolution can be far more difficult. Now that the hurricane is over, he wants to rebuild, but she can't live with the things in the neighborhood that trigger the memories; she wants another child, but he can't face the possible illness of another baby; he wants to reenlist, but she can't imagine living with the risks again. This may be a situation where time, as mentioned previously, can be your ally and postponing the final decision is helpful. When postponing a decision is not possible, it can be helpful to begin by brainstorming every possible solution (even the most extreme) and then deciding which solution takes the least from each partner. The highest priority is the well-being of each partner in the relationship.

Forgiveness. Couples often wonder what part forgiveness plays in resolution. Forgiveness can be a complicated and difficult process, depending upon the nature of the offense. In complex situations, such as infidelity or other betrayals, professional help can be extremely valuable.

However, if we define forgiveness as the ability to go on loving and trusting one's partner, then in small matters forgiveness isn't even thought about—it just happens. In situations where a person's actions have caused anger as well as emotional and physical pain, forgiveness is more likely to happen if that person acknowledges what they have done, and expresses sorrow and a wish to make amends. In such a situation, it is a way to move beyond anger.

Forgiveness does not mean compliance with or acceptance of abuse; nor does it justify holding a partner hostage in punishment or shame. Forgiveness means acceptance of the other's apology and ownership of causing pain. It is about human frailty, trust, and new beginnings.

Optimism. A couple's capacity to reach a resolution—to see the fight or use the disagreement as a way to learn more about their partner—reflects a belief in each other and a capacity to look forward. Looking toward the future with optimism puts negative feelings and reactions into perspective. If you perceive yourselves as a team with a future, then there are few situations or issues that are more important than your future together.

Your Anger Management Plan

Every couple needs a combination of anger prevention, defusing, fair fighting, and resolution strategies in order to deal effectively with anger. Consider what you have read and utilize those ideas and strategies that feel most useful to you. Remember, if you are the only partner reading this book at this point, that is okay. If recovery and rebuilding after this trauma are going to start, someone has to take the first step. The anger pattern between the two of you can't stay the same if one of you changes.

Mutual Recognition of the Need for Professional Help

Recognizing when professional help is needed and taking action to find that help are important commitments for each partner to make. (Even better, try to decide ahead of time that, if either partner ever believes professional help is needed, both will agree to at least seek a consultation. This may help avoid additional conflict when the time comes.) Educating yourself about the signs of the most frequent reactions to trauma that warrant professional assistance can help you to recognize what is going on and make a plan. Here are some of those signs:

- **Substance abuse.** Reliance on alcohol or drugs (both legal and illegal) to regulate mood, ability to relax, and ability to sleep, or any change in substance use or reaction since the trauma, is cause for concern. The connection between alcohol, substance use, anger, domestic abuse, and physical violence is so intense that when associated with post-traumatic stress it can't be ignored.

- **Depression.** Showing disinterest in life, getting too much or too little sleep, overeating or undereating, reduced functionality or inability to work, disinterest in friends or pleasurable activities, negative view of the future, anger and irritability, substance abuse, and suicidal thinking can all be indications of depression.

- **Anger management problems.** Limited tolerance for frustration, which can be indicated by an inability to handle anger without becoming overly reactive, explosive, or violent, suggests a need for outside help. Many uniformed service personnel find anger management groups to be very helpful because such groups recognize and talk about the difficulty of switching from a mission mentality that utilizes anger to civilian life, where this type of anger is problematic.

- **Post-traumatic stress disorder.** Persistence or delayed onset of most of the cluster symptoms of traumatic stress (such as hyperarousal, intrusion, avoidance, and constriction) at least one month after the trauma or the end of the mission can indicate a need for professional help.

Seeking professional help can have a powerful impact on preventing the escalation of destructive anger between partners. It may be a crucial stop on your journey to recovery. Once one or both of you has recognized a need for professional help, it is important to be able to move quickly. It can be helpful to take this step together even if only one of you is experiencing symptoms, since trauma is not something that happens to one person in a couple—it happens to both. Once you meet the professional, leave it to him or her to decide who needs what.

Finding Professional Help

There are a number of ways to find professional help. If you have a trusted family member or friend who has seen a therapist, consider asking him or her for a recommendation. Or you might feel more comfortable asking your family doctor or clergy person for a referral.

There are also a number of ways to get a referral on your own. If you are planning to use your insurance coverage to help pay for the therapist's services, call your provider and get the names of a few professionals in your area who take your insurance. Or you can contact a professional organization such as the American Psychological Association; the National Center for PTSD, which provides information for military personnel and civilians; the American Association of Marriage and Family Therapists; the National Association of Social Workers; or the International Society for Traumatic Stress Studies; all of which can be found online and have links to finding professional help. Also, many professionals post their profile on www.psychologytoday.com, under the heading "Find a Therapist." Regardless of which of these sources you use, try to get a few names to contact. When you contact these therapists, briefly explain why you are seeking help. Do feel free to choose the person with whom you feel most comfortable when talking on the phone. If you meet someone and it does not feel right to one or both of you, keep looking.

Summary

Throughout this chapter, you have seen that the relationship between anger and trauma is common but also complex. The more you understand about the impact of trauma and its physical, psychological, and interpersonal assault on couples, the better you will handle anger together. The fact that you are working to understand and deal with anger is crucial to your recovery and reconnection. You are headed in a positive direction as we turn to intimacy in the next chapter.

4

Dancing in the Dark: Reclaiming Sexual Intimacy

New love is the brightest, and long love is the greatest, but revived love is the tenderest thing known on earth.

—Thomas Hardy

The disruption of intimacy between partners is often part of the collateral damage of trauma. Trauma assaults your sense of self, your view of the world, and your trust in others. It affects you physically and emotionally. It changes your definition of personal safety and your conscious and unconscious desire for closeness. Accordingly, it often changes the sexual intimacy and relationship between you and your partner.

The goal of this chapter is to help you understand how and why trauma disrupts sexual functioning and to offer you strategies for reclaiming, repairing, or reinventing your intimate relationship. It's common for one or both partners to experience a lack of desire, sexual performance problems, or avoidance of intimacy after trauma. However, because one of the insidious effects of trauma is self-blame, shame, and isolation, most people fear that they alone are the only ones with sexual problems, the only ones who can't seem to find each other. As you read this chapter you will find that you are not alone. You will learn about the common sexual issues experienced after trauma and see how they unfold in the lives of other couples.

The Impact of Trauma on Sexual Intimacy

Traumatic events of both a sexual and nonsexual nature can have a devastating impact on a couple's sexual intimacy. In the aftermath of rape, for example, female victims may distrust and avoid intimate relationships and often struggle with difficulties in arousal or physical response (Mills and Turnbull 2004). Though male victims are often at first more angry or dismissive of the rape than women, they, like female victims, suffer increased vulnerability, fear of closeness, shame, and self-blame (Mezey and King 1989).

Sexual changes or reactions resulting from a trauma of a sexual nature are understandable, but there is increasing evidence of sexual and relationship problems in the aftermath of nonsexual trauma (De Silva 2001). Problems with sex and intimacy have been associated with both war exposure and combat trauma. These problems include curtailment of sexual activity, finding sex boring or burdensome, reduced desire, and erectile dysfunction (Solomon 1993; Wilson 1990; Matsakis 1996; Kulka et al. 1990). Studies of male and female Vietnam veterans reveal troubled marital relationships, with 38 percent of the marriages of Vietnam veterans dissolving within six months of their return from Southeast Asia (Kulka et al. 1990; Galovski and Lyons 2003). Sexual difficulties have also been reported by couples who have suffered the loss of a child. The grief from such loss often moves the partners through cycles of shock, numbing, anger, shame, and blame, which can disrupt patterns of relating for months or years (De Silva 2001). In fact, evidence shows that a broad range of traumatic life events, for example, cancer, abortion, miscarriage, auto accidents, and natural disasters, carry with them anxiety, anger, depression, loss, guilt and other feelings, which create difficulties in personal and intimate relationships and often result in sexual difficulties (Mills and Turnbull 2004; De Silva 2001).

Losing Each Other in the Storm

Kim and David, a couple who fled the hurricane, left everything behind and miraculously landed on their feet with a new home in Texas. They even managed to find their dog through one of the online pet rescue organizations. Compared to many, they knew they were very fortunate. Kim was able to transfer her teaching license and though not yet permanently assigned to a position she was called in to work as a substitute most days. Since David's work was Web-based he was able to continue working with very little interruption and not much loss of pay. Why, then, were things so different between them?

David seemed to be living fully in the present, never looking back, seemingly not missing their life in New Orleans at all. It was as if he had totally blocked out the hours they spent stranded on the roof, the old neighbor who died while waiting for help, the misery at the Superdome. Kim wondered how he could forget so easily. Secretly she longed to return to the city she had grown up in. She knew they had been lucky to get out and that New Orleans could flood again, but she missed everything about it. The worst part was her feeling that she could not talk to David about it.

What she didn't know was that most nights David was having nightmares related to the storm. He felt guilty about his failure to protect Kim. It had been his idea to delay leaving, but then it was too late and they ended up trapped, enduring the hours of waiting, not knowing what would happen, and fearing for their lives.

During the day he could keep his feelings walled off if he kept working and making efforts to connect in their new community. He put his energy into looking ahead and speaking positively about the future, wanting never again to disappoint Kim or put her in harm's way. Nights were difficult, though. He felt embarrassed that he wasn't coping, and he was unable to share his memories or nightmares with Kim. He felt guilty and inadequate as a man and as a husband. Adding to his secret fears was his worry about his sexual performance. When they were newly relocated he had initiated sex a few times, only to find that despite his longing for Kim he simply could not sustain an erection. Kim was both understanding and reassuring, but the difficulty increased his feelings of inadequacy and stopped him from reaching out to her. As a result, Kim was left feeling rejected and became silently resentful and ultimately depressed. She started to feel that she had lost everything. How could they connect with their new life if they had lost the ability to connect with each other?

Never before had secrets separated them. Pillow talk— sharing confidences, including fears and hopes—had always been part of their private life together. Now, it was as if their bed were filled with ghosts from the past: images of the roof, the water, the Superdome, the friends and family they had left behind. Even though they were safe, they could not find one another.

Understanding Trauma's Impact

The reason why traumatic events disrupt and compromise intimacy and sexual functioning is that trauma is by definition a life-threatening event engendering fear and helplessness and calling forth the body's stress responses. Symptoms of hyperarousal, intrusion, and constriction or numbing reflect the body and mind's reaction to danger. Whether such symptoms last for only a few weeks, emerge after six months, or develop into PTSD, they often have an impact on sexual relating. In addition, other reactions such as depression, grief, and anxiety often coexist with trauma symptoms and add to difficulties with intimate connection.

We certainly see evidence of this difficulty in the case of David and Kim. Despite his efforts to wall off his feelings about all that had happened, David had memories, feelings of guilt, and nightmares that he kept to himself rather than trusting Kim to understand. He reacted to his sexual difficulties by avoiding sex as well as any discussion about it, thereby preventing Kim's involvement and the possibility of reconnecting and perhaps improving his sexual functioning. Kim, like many victims of natural disaster, was grateful for their safe relocation but suffered from the sudden physical and emotional loss of her home and all the personal resources, friends, and community associated with it. Not wanting to upset David, Kim kept her experience of loss, her sexual desire, and her feelings of rejection to herself and became depressed.

Like many couples faced with unexpected life events, David and Kim couldn't make sense of what had happened to their connection. They didn't understand the impact of trauma on their sexual relationship or how to address it. Let's take a closer look at how post-traumatic response symptoms and depression affect sexual relating.

The Impact of Post-traumatic Symptoms on Sexual Intimacy

Each of the three primary trauma cluster symptoms of hyperarousal, reexperiencing, and numbing and constriction is likely to have an effect on sexual intimacy. The disruption caused by each may be somewhat different as will the strategy that may be most helpful in working through it. Each of these is discussed and described below.

Hyperarousal. Hyperarousal is the persistent expectation of being in danger. This translates into symptoms such as the inability to relax, exaggerated startle response, sleep difficulties, anger, irritability, and hypersensitivity to stimulation, all of which compromise intimacy. It is difficult to feel sexual if you or your partner is frightened and hypervigilant about sound or touch. If exhaustion becomes a factor, or if sleep schedules are out of whack (perhaps one of you tries to sleep and the other attempts to avoid sleep by surfing the Web or watching TV), romance is compromised. Spending time together relaxing, engaging in pillow talk, listening to music, or watching a sitcom together may become difficult and tense and you may ultimately avoid these kinds of activities. Similarly, hypersensitivity often makes erotic or intimate activities like massage, showering together, or just spooning, which you may have shared before, too uncomfortable. Anxiety may well interfere with sexual performance, and the letting-go that is necessary for sexual release and orgasm is understandably difficult to achieve in a state of hypervigilance and tension.

Exercise: Hyperarousal

Most couples can benefit from relaxation. This strategy will not only help with some of the symptoms of hyperarousal described previously but also reduce general stress and tension. We invite you to try it together.

Double Deep Breathing

Goal: Relaxation

Rationale: You can't be physically relaxed and stressed at the same time. Controlled breathing techniques are quick and fairly easy ways of lowering physiological stress. With anxiety, a person will often engage in shallow breathing, which brings less oxygen to the bloodstream, in turn setting off warning signals that lead to more adrenaline and increased shallow breathing. Controlled deep breathing provides a way to move your body out of a hyperaroused and anxious state.

Description: You can either sit up side by side or lie down next to each other. One of you can give the directions aloud: "We are going to place our hands on our laps, or next to us if lying down, or gently hold hands. We will close our eyes and slowly inhale to the count of four, feeling our abdomens expand. Then we are going to slow exhale from our noses to the count of four until we have let all the air out. We will continue to do this for three minutes." (You might want to place a clock in easy view or play a relaxing song—the average song is about three minutes long.)

Variation: Try again using imagery. Many people find that positive imagery adds to the experience of relaxed breathing. Give the directions out loud as follows: "We are going to picture a scene where we would like to be—a beach, a forest, a lakeside. We will try to imagine what we feel as we lie there, what we see, what we hear, what we smell."

Guidelines: After three minutes, or when you are ready to stop if you have tried it again or added imagery, slowly open your eyes and take a minute to mentally come back to the room and each other. Look into each other's eyes, touch in whatever way feels comfortable to both of you, and take turns telling your partner about the relaxing place you visited. Feel the deepening of intimacy that comes with this exercise. Repeat, practice, and enjoy.

Intrusion or Reexperiencing. Symptoms of intrusion or reexperiencing can trap you in the feelings and images of the traumatic moment. The imprint of the trauma can be experienced as nightmares, flashbacks, intrusive memories, or sensations that interfere with the feelings of safety and relaxation that are necessary for affection, sexual touch, and arousal. Such symptoms can be triggered by sounds, light, or the movement or touch of your partner, and they usually result in fear and caution on the part of both partners. As with David, discussed in the last example, the partner who is having intrusive symptoms is often self-critical and embarrassed, and becomes secretive or avoidant. The other partner often feels rejected or helpless, as Kim did.

If you both have experienced a traumatic event, like the death of a child or a natural disaster, each of you may choose not to disclose nightmares or memories, in order to avoid upsetting your partner. However, the result of this is isolation, and you miss the opportunity to use your connection as an antidote to your stress and traumatic response.

If you are trying to reconnect with your partner and you are having trouble because of memories, flashbacks, or ruminations about the traumatic events, consider using the next strategy.

Exercise: Intrusion and Reexperiencing

Mental Focusing for Two

Goal: To reduce anxiety, increase ability to relax, reclaim pillow talk, and use combined mental energy to move thinking into something positive, enjoyable, and maybe even fun and humorous

Rationale: Mental focusing techniques and positive imagery can be used by either partner to reduce negative or intrusive thoughts that emerge when you are trying to relax or fall asleep. When used by a couple, they may help lower the anxiety and lessen the ruminating that can interfere with the relaxing, cuddling, caressing, and responsiveness that lead to sexual connection. These techniques take you "off task" by shifting to a positive focus and inviting sharing and playing together. We recommend that you try them while lying down next to each other.

Description: "Name That Title"—Choose a category that matches both of your interests (such as movies, songs, sports teams, or books) and a word, and ask your partner to name a movie, song, sports team, or book with that word in its title. For example, one partner says, "Name a movie with the word 'pink' in it." The other might reply, "*The Pink Panther.*" Try this out a number of times in different categories.

"Remember When"—Together, name three movies (or TV shows, songs, restaurants, or other things) that you both saw, heard, visited, and so on in the 1960s, '70s, '80s, '90s, and 2000s.

Avoidance, Numbing, and Constriction. The traumatic stress symptoms of avoidance, numbing, and constriction are conscious and unconscious attempts to avoid feelings and body states associated with the trauma. They are very disruptive to intimacy because they leave you unable to feel or even to know what you feel. You may feel confused and fearful that you don't love your partner, because you can't seem to feel the way you felt before the trauma. Sometimes you may avoid intimacy because it stirs up feelings, and all feelings have become unsafe for you. However, attempting to selectively wall off negative feelings never works. Attempting to keep a partner out of your pain by maintaining your distance only keeps him or her disconnected from you—something that prevents the recovery of safe and positive feelings and is usually more painful than experiencing the feelings you may be avoiding.

If you or your partner feels emotionally numb or is not sure how to reconnect sexually, start by spending some low-pressure, nonthreatening time together to rebuild your connection.

Exercise: Numbing and Avoidance

The Coffee Break Connection

Goal: To reconnect with your partner in a safe, gradual way that fosters communication and closeness

Rationale: Reconnecting by taking very small, predictable steps offers a safe way to begin.

Description: Make a commitment to meet together for lunch, dinner, or just coffee at a certain time and place away from your other responsibilities every week. You can travel together to your meeting place (the park, a nearby cafe, a local diner, or other place) or plan to meet there. At first this may feel awkward—you may have no idea what to talk about. To help the conversation move along, bring the newspaper and look through the articles on news events, sports, or movies. Discuss a movie or event you may want to attend. Spend some time planning something together, like a vacation, barbecue, or future date. As you continue to meet in this way, you may begin to save things to discuss during your "coffee break." Setting aside a time to just have a cup of coffee together sends a message of interest, special feelings, even desire. It is a powerful first step to being close again without feeling guilt or pressure.

Variation: After a period of time, if the coffee break starts to feel too routine, try varying the location or try listening to music together. Music actually has the potential to facilitate feelings. Daniel Levitin (2006), author of *This Is Your Brain on Music*, tells us that music changes heart and respiration rates, stirs memories, and can even raise levels of the hormone dopamine (one of the hormones involved in sexual arousal and sexual interest). If your goal is to move from numbing and constriction to feeling again, then listening to music may be a way to help you accomplish this. Make a CD of songs you remember from when you and your partner first met, or grab your partner's current favorite CD, and put it on in the car the next time you go out together. You don't even have to say anything. Just enjoy the feelings. You are feeling your way past the trauma.

The Impact of Depression on Sexual Intimacy

Depression is a common response in the aftermath of trauma and is often experienced in addition to PTSD symptoms. Characterized by lethargy, loss of interest, lowered self-esteem, inability to experience pleasure, difficulties with sleeping and eating, negative perspective, and social withdrawal, depression often interferes with sexual functioning and intimate relating (Baldwin 2001). The inability to desire, respond to, or relate to one's partner often adds to the lowered self-esteem and guilt people experience with depression. Further complicating the sexual issues with depression is the fact that a number of medications used to address depression symptoms actually reduce sexual interest in women and increase sexual performance difficulties in men. Although these side effects can be handled with medication, for a time couples may feel caught up in a no-win situation.

If one of you is dealing with depression in a way that disrupts or limits sexual connection, approach the situation together: acknowledge that the side effects are typical with this medication, stay close to each other by participating in other recreational activities, provide support by helping each other stick to regular sleep and exercise schedules, and try some of the strategies discussed in this chapter. Your efforts are likely to reduce blame and increase intimacy between you.

Communicating About Your Sexual Relationship After Trauma

David and Kim's experience shows that not communicating about the feelings and symptoms interfering with intimacy may be as damaging as the symptoms themselves.

Traumatic events are so psychologically disruptive that they often dominate a couple's every moment, or they become the elephant in the room that both partners avoid discussing. Sometimes the traumatic event polarizes a couple so that one ruminates about it and the other minimizes it. In all cases, trauma has center stage, and the partners stop communicating with each other and being present to each other in the moment. When trauma stops a couple from being confidants, it jeopardizes their connection as lovers.

Guidelines to Enhance Intimate Communication

As lovers, you and your partner have an exclusive bond that connects you physically, verbally, and emotionally. The following questions and information are intended to be used as a guideline as you think about and discuss your current and future relationship as confidants and lovers.

- Do you wish to be sexual with your partner in the future?

  Communicating about sexual issues starts with communicating the wish to be together in a sexual way even if this wish can't be acted upon at the present time. This may seem like a simple and obvious concept, but when a couple is seriously working on intimacy it is a powerful first step. It often relieves guilt for not feeling sexual, and it may reduce fear of rejecting or being rejected. Letting your partner know that you still want to be with him or her sexually is a way of connecting and setting an important mutual goal. Sometimes a partner may say he is uncertain about whether he wants to be sexual again, and it is worth accepting this as an honest and sincere statement of communication. Keep in mind that uncertainty and fear of never being the same can be part of the overlay of depression and PTSD. For this reason, it is worth proceeding with the other questions and suggestions.

- Has the inability to talk about the trauma, or too much talk about the trauma, kept you at a distance from each other?

  Whether you have been talking excessively or not at all about the traumatic event, you may not yet have made *meaning* of the trauma together in a way that has allowed you to go on. To help you begin to find a meaning in it, we recommend clearly sharing your version of the trauma with your partner. Whether you suffered the same trauma or only one of you directly faced the event, you both have a version of what happened to you as individuals and as a couple. The feeling of *being known by* and *knowing* your partner is necessary for intimacy, and this is what is thrown off course by trauma. It is common for people recovering from a trauma to say, "I don't know this stranger I'm living with," or "I can't be who I was." This is a step toward recapturing the feeling of *knowing* and *being known*.

* To share your version of what happened, make time for both partners to communicate their version of the traumatic event to the other. We suggest that the other will listen without interruption (even if you think you know it, have heard it, or have said it before). This conversation can be short or long. It can be done once or in a number of planned sittings. Or you can write it in letters that you write to each other and read side by side or e-mails that you print and share. Remember that it is not about the details. It is about what you have been alone with. It is about reinstating your partner as your confient.

* Are you aware of your sexual needs and those of your partner?

  Communicating sexual awareness is a way of getting comfortable with talking about sexual feelings. There are three ingredients to safely communicating about sexual needs: (1) the ability to talk authentically, (2) the ability to feel heard, and (3) having respect for each partner's differences. To begin talking about sexual needs, follow these steps:

  1. Each of you can take turns communicating your own sexual and emotional needs. For example, you might say something like, "I miss you and want to have sex with you," "I love you and I don't want to lose you, but I'm too anxious to be sexual," or "I would like you to be more seductive so I can start to feel sexual again."

  2. After one of you has spoken, the listener should repeat what his or her partner has shared. Repeating is a way of confirming what has been said. It is a way to send the message, "It is okay that you have shared this, and I have heard what you said."

  3. Reverse roles. If you were the listener, you now share your sexual needs and feelings with your partner, who now listens and then repeats what has been said.

  4. Both of you should allow yourselves time to process what has been said: "Let's talk again tomorrow." This takes the pressure off and really allows processing to happen.

Of course, we hope that your communications about your sexual feelings will lead to intimate times together, but for the purposes of this exercise it is best to just talk. This will allow sex to become possible and special in your relationship. Accordingly, communicating sexual needs and awareness does not necessitate immediate sexual response to what the other has shared; nor does it mean surrendering your needs or solving your partner's worries. You are simply working on being confidants. The ability to say something and have the other just hear it, respect it, and think about it is a crucial aspect of sexual communication and reconnecting.

* Are you giving yourselves time for pillow talk (side-by-side relaxing and talking about whatever comes to mind)?

Engaging in pillow talk somewhere, somehow, is an important aspect of sexual communication. Try it. Share something that is on your mind at a relaxed, intimate time with your partner. It might precede or follow sexual connection, but it does not require you to be sexual at that time. It does not matter if you are lying down together or if one is sitting at the edge of a bed. It simply means being together.

Reserved for no one but the two of you, pillow talk often unlocks the walled-off fears and feelings that cause the sexual disconnect between partners.

Special Issues for Couples Affected by Sexual Trauma

A firefighter and a nurse, respectively, Danny and Meg would often talk about the events in life that people never see coming. That's what happened the morning she was raped.

Danny and Meg were a perfect match from the day they were introduced at the finish line of a 5K race. Married for a year, juggling job shifts and lots of mutual friends, the "newlyweds," as their friends called them, loved their life and couldn't keep their hands off each other. One morning after work, Meg decided to go for a run at the nearby high-school track. Having changed into running gear at the hospital, she pulled up behind the school, put on her iPod, and headed along the edge of the grass to the track. By the time she realized someone was behind her, he was on top of her. She tried to scream, but he put his hand on her mouth and pulled her sweater up over her head. Later, she wouldn't be able to tell if her instincts had told her not to fight or if she had been frozen with fear. She knew she would forever be grateful to the track team kids whose car pulled up within minutes, causing the guy to pull away and take off back to his car. Seeing her and realizing what had happened, the kids called 911 and later identified his car for the police.

Danny got the call and met her at the hospital. She knew the routine; she even knew the nurse who did the rape evaluation. But it was the look on Danny's face that made her cry. They both cried. Determined to get through this, they both took a week off just to be together to relax and feel safe. Meg went back to work and found a support group.

Returning to lovemaking was a problem. Both were unsure of themselves. Danny had been hesitant to resume sexual relating during the second week, and Meg's support group had encouraged her to go slowly and recondition herself to Danny's safe touch, but Meg was determined not to let the guy who raped her take away their lovemaking. The problem was that, despite her wishes and their initial physical connections, at some point Meg would burst into tears and pull away. Feeling guilty and helpless, Danny would reassure Meg that they needed time. Sometimes she would get angry and blame Danny, only to apologize later. After a few times, both agreed to just wait, but they felt quite lost.

Coping Together After Sexual Trauma

Although 15 percent of the general population who have endured a trauma experience some PTSD, 50 percent of all women who have been raped experience it. And male victims often report experiencing long-term crises with their sexual orientation and sense of masculinity, which compromise their desire and sexual relating (Walker, Archer, and Davies 2005).

As you can see, what makes sexual trauma more complicated and in some ways more devastating to a couple's intimacy is that it disrupts a warm, loving resource for recovery. That sensual connection and sexual exchange, ordinarily so healing, is the very context of the trauma and a trigger for retraumatization.

Fortunately, if a person who has faced sexual trauma is in a committed relationship, he or she is at an advantage for recovery, because a trusting, intimate relationship is the best resource and the most potent antidote to the pain and suffering associated with sexual trauma.

Guidelines for Couples Recovering from Sexual Trauma

The trauma may have happened to one of you, but the impact on your sexual relationship undoubtedly affects you both. The following recommendations can be helpful to the two of you.

Recognition and Acceptance of Common Reactions of Victims. Symptom clusters of PTSD are very common after rape and include the following:

* Hyperarousal, including startle response, sleep disturbance, fear of darkness, irritability, anger, and panic attacks

* Reexperiencing or intrusions, including nightmares; flashbacks; body triggers of sight, touch, smell, and sound

* Numbing and avoidance, including feeling frozen; avoidance of sexual arousal; lack of arousal in females; inability to sustain an erection in males; withdrawal from friends, partner, and formerly enjoyed activities

* Symptoms that flare up as intimacy with a partner is contemplated or attempted, for example, feelings of nausea and vomiting before or after sex, or feelings of sexual arousal causing flashbacks to the attack during intimate moments

* Feelings of self-blame and shame, sometimes leading the victim to force themselves to be sexual, as Meg did

(Sometimes victims begin to engage in promiscuous behavior as an unconscious defense to the feelings of helplessness and victimization associated with the assault.)

* Gender confusion and a view of sex as dirty or disgusting

Recognition and Acceptance of Common Partner Reactions. It's common for a person whose partner has been raped to suffer from secondary post-traumatic stress. These partners often experience horror, helplessness, fear, and rage at the violent assault and possible near-death experience of a significant person in their life. They may also suffer from the same symptom clusters (hyperarousal, intrusion and numbing, constriction and avoidance). For example, often the partner struggles with rage toward the attacker; hypersensitivity and caution about triggering traumatic responses in their partner; flashbacks to details and descriptions given by their partner victim; numbing and disinterest in sex and sexual performance difficulties; and self-blame, shame, and fear of being pitied.

Such partners may feel disenfranchised—not entitled to have feelings of their own in reaction to what their partner has experienced. Often they may feel irrational guilt for not having protected their partner, and they may experience feelings of helplessness after the event. Feelings of compassion and sensitivity can simultaneously lead to fear of sex with their partner and feelings of depression, both recognized and unrecognized.

Making a Couple Recovery Plan. Accepting that all of these responses are understandable does not mean you must surrender to them. It means that you acknowledge them and help yourself and your partner address them with specific strategies over time, such as the following:

Reestablishing trust and a safe physical connection together. Remain physically close together in activities that are soothing but less directly sexual, such as cuddling, massage, showering, or soaking in a hot tub. Make use of the positive associations to the senses. Turn on some music and dance, attend live music concerts, or just do chores around the house to a favorite CD. Choose fragrances and candles that you both enjoy, and use them in the house during times when you are together doing something relaxing.

Research on the impact of rape on sexual satisfaction suggests that experiences of affection are less associated with the rape than overtly sexual activity and thus are more easily accepted by the victim in the first few months following the assault (Feldman-Summers, Gordon, and Meagher 1979). If you are the partner of someone who has been sexually assaulted, be sure to show your care and love through physical acts such as hugs, holding your partner's hand, light kisses, and touches to the back, waist, and arms to show affection that is not overtly sexual.

The goal is to recondition your partner's body awareness—touch, sight, smell, and sound—to respond positively to what is safe and pleasurable with a trusted partner. Review the couple's strategies for hyperarousal, reexperiencing, and numbing and avoidance described earlier in this chapter and together consider which one you might try.

Reframing sexuality as a safe and shared experience. Develop a stop-and-go code as you return to lovemaking, using a signal such as a touch on the shoulder to mean "stop." Either partner can use this signal to stop at any time during intimate encounters. When either partner gives the "stop" signal, the other partner can ask questions to find out what his or her needs are, such as, "Do you want to stop? Are you feeling okay? Would you like me to do something differently?"

Plan a backup strategy that you can use if one partner wants the sexual encounter to stop. Consider just hugging, cuddling up together under the blankets, taking a bath or shower together, or putting on music. Be gentle and remind each other that you are together and you are safe.

Using strategies like these to reframe sexuality in your relationship is very different from just avoiding sexual behavior altogether. You are taking steps toward being *safe and sexual* again.

The Impact of Trauma on Sexual Desire

A common complaint after trauma is that sexual desire is easily thwarted—one of you is just about to consider making a connection and the slightest thing throws it off. The wish, ability, or desire to connect may be fragile, but that does not mean it is not there. You may be experiencing similar disruptions with other activities. The plan to watch TV, having a meal, or enjoy a car ride together may well be thrown off by physical pain, fatigue, anxiety, or the needs of your children, but these are sometimes better tolerated than sexual disruptions. Accordingly, it is important to recognize that losing the moment is not evidence that your partner lacks sexual desire. It's just that you are readjusting many aspects of your life right now.

Lack of desire is complex and difficult to define and may reflect factors that have nothing to do with your real feelings for each other. Understanding more about the nature of male and female sexual desire may help you put your responses and expectations in perspective and make it easier to reclaim your sexuality.

Understanding Sexual Desire in Your Partner

According to Elaine Hatfield (1988), women develop a "person centered" or relationship orientation to sexuality. For them, the goal of sex is to express affection to another in a committed relationship. Men have a "body centered" orientation toward sex. For them, the goal of sex is physical gratification. A study of the gender differences in what is desired in sexual relationships found that the top two desires for married men were for partners to initiate sex more and be more seductive. The top two desires for married women were for partners to talk lovingly more often—and be more seductive (Hatfield et al. 1989). It is striking that both men and women want their partners to be more seductive. However, they want this in different ways. This is consistent with neuro-physiological findings that in men the desire for sex is physically driven and arousal is most prominently stirred by visual cues, while in women sexual desire is motivated by the wish for intimacy and connection with the partner. Essentially both want to be sexual with each other, but both use different cues for arousal and desire. So, for example, he would love her to wear sexy lingerie and she would love him to tell her what she means to him.

The wish for your partner to know your intimate needs is common and may be even greater under the stress and strain of post-traumatic recovery. You may have very little patience with your partner's inability to read your mind about wanting to be touched, wanting a particular type of seductive behavior, or wanting to be left alone. When partners start keeping score of these kinds of missed cues out of fear of the other's rejection or loss of interest, they create distance, misunderstanding, and the lack of interest and avoidance they fear. Desire may still exist, but they haven't developed enough mutual understanding or a safe-enough place (physically or psychologically) to be together.

The Case of a Lost Sexual Self

Greg and Ellyn each considered the early part of their relationship to be "hot." They had met in their mid-twenties and had found they had a lot in common as they worked to build their careers while also holding onto their more carefree college lifestyle. Initially they did everything together when they were not at work. They described their love life as extremely satisfying and their intimacy seemed only to deepen. The passing years brought kids, additional responsibilities, and family and professional demands, all competing for scarce time. At first this took its toll on the relationship, but they gradually found ways to make time to be alone together, even occasionally playing hooky from their jobs when the kids were in school to try to re-create their early carefree days.

Then came Greg's heart attack. Ellyn would never forget the phone call she received at work, the mad drive to the hospital, the hours of not knowing. It made no sense. Greg was only forty-four. He went to the gym regularly and ate well. Their kids were young; they had their whole life ahead of them.

Greg did pull through, with the recuperation taking a number of months and turning their worlds upside down. Ellyn took a leave of absence from work and stayed home to take care of Greg and everything else. She stopped going to her exercise class and gained twenty-five pounds. Meanwhile, Greg worked hard to regain his strength but was sullen and withdrawn except with the kids. Silently he examined his finances, put papers in order, and worried about dying.

Eventually both went back to work, feeling lucky that they had pulled through. The rhythm of their life began to approximate that of old times, with one clear exception: after six months there had been no sexual contact between them. In the past this was unheard of. Ellyn wondered why, but she realized she was afraid of what might happen if Greg exerted himself too much. She hated when he went back to vigorous gym workouts, regardless of what the doctor had said. She also hated her own body; she felt fat and unattractive and certainly not sexual. She assumed that Greg could not possibly find her desirable looking the way she did. In fact, there was some truth to that. It wasn't just the weight, but Greg was aware that Ellyn was different. Her whole demeanor had changed; she had lost her playful flirtatiousness. There was something about the way she moved—it was more like a nurse or a mother, not a wife or playmate. He felt guilty for feeling this way. "Look how much she has sacrificed for me," he thought. "She stayed home, gave up a likely promotion, handled everything until I was back on my feet. Leave it alone; perhaps in time things will get back to the way they were."

Turning Trauma Bonds into Intimacy Bonds

In the face of near-death experiences, partners often become stuck in some version of a trauma bond that interferes with intimacy. In this case, Ellyn stayed fixed in her worrying about losing Greg and in so doing seemed to lose herself. She gained weight, disliked how she looked, and gave up her young, sexy identity. Because she was overly focused on looking at him, she could not see herself in the way she used to, and neither could he.

Ellyn's trauma bond with Greg was keeping them both stuck and without the freedom to move beyond the trauma into the future. Some couples cling to each other with fear and worry, some partners avoid the other in order to circumvent the dependency they need but fear, and some, like Ellyn, find themselves giving up their role of intimate partner to become a permanent caretaker, whether it's needed or not. In this case, Ellyn and Greg needed to separate from their identification with the trauma so they could rediscover themselves as lovers.

If you want to change the way you are relating and reestablish your intimate bond, you don't need to start in bed. Research tells us that most partners share three domains of expressive communication:

- **Companionship**—being with and doing things with your partner

- **Empathy**—listening to, caring about, and understanding each other

- **Physical connection**—expressing love through touch, caress, and sexual intercourse (Scanzoni and Scanzoni 1988)

It has been found that an increase in the quality of one type of expressive communication increases the quality of the others. Couples who spend leisure time together usually find things to talk about, which helps them understand each other and feel more empathy toward each other. And, since partners tend to talk about personal issues before and after sex, sexual connection may actually enhance attachment and communication (Cupach and Comstock 1990).

Strategy: Enhancing Desire

- **Make your desire clear.** If you make it clear in some way to your partner that you don't want to *just be friends* then it hardly matters where you start, as long as you are making an honest effort to understand and be compassionate toward your partner. Chances are, you are going to feel and become more sexual whether you are fishing, talking over coffee, or dancing in the dark. Consider exploring some of the strategies we've outlined in this chapter so far, such as discussing your sexual needs and feelings, making time to be with your partner on a regular basis, or doing a shared relaxation and visualization exercise.

- **Recognize your partner's sexual receptivity.** Often, understanding sexual desire and sexual receptivity help couples put their fears and expectations into perspective. Rosemary Basson's (2003) insight into sexual desire offers an understanding that may prompt curiosity and collaboration rather than actual or anticipated criticism between partners. She suggests that in the beginning of a romantic relationship there is often a similarity in the sexual drive or interest, probably driven by the neurochemistry associated with both partners' excitement. With time, however, the differences in men and women become more prominent. Basson offers a different way of thinking about *sexual receptivity*: a partner's tendency to not think about or initiate sex does not equal a lack of receptivity, enjoyment, and passion. As Ellyn and Greg discovered, trauma often leaves one feeling self-conscious, physically different, and emotionally unsure. The known self who interacted with the known partner is gone. Recognizing that a hesitation to initiate sex or act sexy does not equate to a lack of desire or interest can be crucial in recovering intimacy after trauma. In other words, the fact that Ellyn does not look like or act like her old sexual self does not mean she does not want to be sexual or would not have responded if Greg had initiated. In the same way, the fact that Greg may have been less affectionate with Ellyn than his old sexual self does not mean that he would not have responded to her advances. In fact, if Ellyn were to initiate some sexual advances, this might have taken the image of her as *caretaker* off the screen. Once started, a positive sexual experience actually becomes the trigger of desire for more connection.

When it seems that desire has been dampened by trauma, the question to ask is not "What is wrong with him or her?" but "How can I invite sexual connection in a way that will help him or her be more receptive to it?"

■ **Use your neurochemistry.** Given the balance of testosterone, estrogen, and other bodily ingredients, as well as social circumstances and a host of other factors (such as illness, combat stress, fatigue, age, fear, thoughts, images, associations, and past history) that play a role in sexual desire, sometimes a couple can outsmart chemistry to reclaim their sexuality. Usually if both partners join forces they can do it. Just thinking about making a plan to do this can trip anticipation and desire in the body and brain. One of the reasons that vacations, unpredictable reactions, changes in patterns, novelty, exhilarating sports, and exercise enhance a couple's sexual desire and responsiveness is that these situations actually change neurochemistry. They stimulate hormones related to sexual desire, excitement, and arousal. You really will feel more sexual in a beautiful hotel room or in your brother-in-law's tiny guest room because they are different and unfamiliar and you are together in a new way, just like you were toward the beginning of your relationship!

■ **Couple's interest and excitement list.** Try experiencing the impact of neurochemistry on desire. Each of you can make a list of places, activities, or changes in patterns that you would be willing to try. When you are both ready, compare and discuss your lists and then write a new list that includes some items from each of your lists—but only those that you both are okay with. Consider marking your calendar with some of these places, activities, or changes in your daily activity patterns. For example, you might schedule dance lessons, a beach date, a visit to a local motel, shopping for underwear, a gambling weekend, and so on.

The Impact of Combat on Sexual Relating

We know that many veterans develop sexual problems and suffer from relationship and intimacy difficulties with partners in the aftermath of combat and war (Solomon 1993; Wilson 1990; Figley 2005). These difficulties can manifest themselves in lack of sexual desire, erectile dysfunction, lack of interest, and avoidance of intimacy. Veterans may have a wonderful homecoming and reunion with their partner, only to become affected by the onset of these sexual problems. These common problems are often unexpected by veterans and their partners, causing them to feel anxious, guilty, damaged, and rejected when the joy and relief of being reunited begins to erode.

> *When Matt, a thirty-five-year-old guardsman, finally came home after nineteen months and two tours in Iraq, Cathy, his wife, could not have been more thrilled. On maternity leave from teaching at the time he was deployed, Cathy had been living on the edge of hope, communicating by e-mail with Matt and sending pictures of their baby daughter so he could watch her grow. When Matt returned, Missy was over two years old, a little cautious but looking very much like her dad. Grateful to be with his girls, Matt resumed his work as an electrician and*

he and Cathy enjoyed reconnecting with family and friends. The first month was underscored with excitement and the desire to be together. Although it was the first time they had to work romance around the demands of a two-year-old, they fell into each other's arms with more than the old passion. Surprising to both, this did not seem to last. As time went on, readjustment actually became more difficult, a situation Cathy had heard about at a military family support center but didn't understand. She found that for some reason she and Matt slowly became more distant. Sure, they could sit in the kitchen and delight in spending time with Missy, but as they entered Matt's fourth month home there seemed to be less affection and sexual connection. Cathy started to worry that maybe Matt thought she had been unfaithful while he was away and actually asked him about this. He laughed and said he didn't think he had much competition, which actually made them both laugh and draw closer, but it didn't last. A few times Cathy suggested that she would wait up for him or invited him to watch late-night TV like they had in the old days, but Matt would say he was kind of wired and was going to do paperwork or surf the Internet. When Matt did come to bed he sometimes wanted sex, but it seemed different—more rushed, with less of the caressing or cuddling that she loved. Cathy didn't say anything and went through the motions. She knew Matt was having a hard time relaxing and needed time. She also knew that they had been arguing more lately; he was constantly checking on her and the baby or warning her about the dangers of shopping alone or going to the gym at night. This lecturing seemed overbearing and made her crazy—she had lived without him for nineteen months and had kept herself safe all that time. Then there was the night she went down to check on him and saw that he was looking at some pornography. Matt quickly turned it off without saying anything, and she went upstairs feeling like she was married to a stranger.

Matt himself felt like he was on another planet. He loved Cathy and the baby but knew that emotionally he was not yet home. When he had first come home, he just wanted to be with Cathy as he had imagined thousands of times, and those first few weeks were just like that, better than their honeymoon. What was strange was that the farther he got from Iraq and the less he talked about it, the more he thought about it. He remembered a captain saying, "You'd better talk a lot to each other here, because when you get back home, no one will understand." Matt didn't think he could or should talk to Cathy about the things he remembered. He actually feared that if she really knew what had happened, how horrific war could be, she would not want to be close to him. At the same time, he resented her for thinking he was the same guy she had married and for assuming that he should just slide back into their life. He was unsure of how to do normal life again. He couldn't help worrying that something bad was going to happen when she went to the gym at night. Why couldn't she just listen to him and stay home? And he was having trouble feeling sexual with her. At least with the porn he could put everything else out of his mind and feel aroused. He felt guilty that a few times he had actually started masturbating to porn and then had gone to bed to be with Cathy. She didn't say anything those nights, just like she didn't say anything when she had walked in on him looking at porn. What was he supposed to say to her about the porn? He was back home, but he couldn't find himself or Cathy.

Matt and Cathy, like many veterans and their partners, were mystified that as time passed their readjustment became more difficult and the early excitement of their reunion waned. In addition to dealing with hypervigilance, reflected in his concern about her goings and comings, Matt was struggling with a mix of intrusive thoughts and numbed-out feelings that made him turn to pornography. Although this provided him some temporary relief from these thoughts and feelings, we can see that his solution kept him feeling guilty, desperate, and at a distance from Cathy. She, in turn, was left feeling worried, rejected, and stunned by his use of porn.

Understanding and Dealing with Pornography

Pornography, which includes adult and sexually oriented DVDs, magazines, books, and websites, is a passing curiosity for some, a source of pleasure for others, and a serious addiction for still others. For some couples the casual use of pornography by one or both partners is acceptable, sometimes pleasurable, and not disruptive to their sexual connection. For others, as in the case of Matt and Cathy, the awareness of a partner's use of pornography generates distrust, discomfort, and betrayal. Often, the awareness of a partner's porn use is followed by judgment, guilt, shame, and lowered self-esteem in both partners. In all cases when pornography becomes an addiction (such that it is all consuming and cannot be given up despite job, health, legal, and relationship consequences), it destroys partners' ability to connect and makes sexual intimacy with a partner impossible.

The Relationship of Trauma and Pornography

The use of pornography is not uncommon in the aftermath of trauma, because, like alcohol and drugs, porn offers temporary relief from the post-traumatic stress symptoms of hyperarousal, intrusions, and numbing. Matt was using it to distract himself from intrusive memories of Iraq and to deal with his difficulty with sexual desire and arousal. The downside of pornography is that it leaves out the real partner, both emotionally and physically. It may sexually stimulate Matt, but it forecloses on the possibility of his sharing authentic feelings with Cathy and their ability to work on sexual desire and arousal together. Even if, as is the case with many vets, it was a solution to loneliness and deprivation when deployed, reliance upon it at home keeps Matt lonely and deprived. Feelings of shame or self-blame that may make a partner use porn are often exacerbated by the secrets kept or exposed about its use.

Couple's Guidelines for Dealing with Pornography

1. If you are aware that your partner is using or has used pornography, or your partner is quite open about it and wants to continue, ask to talk about it. Rather than judging or condemning, or feeling rejected or angry, try being curious. Let your partner know that you want to understand what this means. Both of you might take the time to actually answer the questions, "What does porn mean to each of us individually? How does its use relate to our situation?" You might ask, "Why do you view it?" You could also ask yourselves, "What impact do we each feel it has on our sexual connection, and our love life?" For example, had Cathy asked Matt what he was viewing

and why, in a way that showed concern or interest, he might have been able to share his struggle, and they might have been able to come to a solution to their sexual problems.

2. Come to a mutual understanding of what will work for you as a couple. This does not mean finding an immediate solution. In fact, as we have said earlier, take some time to just process what the other shares about the meaning and impact of pornography on you as a couple. Is it being used for escape, out of habit, for arousal, for attention? Live with it for a bit, think about it, and put it in perspective. Make a plan to sit and share what each of you took away from the first conversation and your thoughts about it. The goal is not to gain control. The goal is to understand in a way that invites trust and connection. The plan or mutual understanding that you come to will only work if it does not impair your intimacy. For example, some couples agree to stop using pornography and then find that there is actually less interest in or need for it as the relationship improves. Other couples choose to focus more on the honesty of sharing what both might be doing rather than making a definite rule against using pornography.

3. If you or your partner cannot stop using pornography and any of the aspects of your life together are jeopardized as a result, then it is important to seek professional help. And, as with other addictions, the support of a partner can play a powerful role in recovery. Often a twelve-step program with an outside sponsor as backup support is a valuable arrangement, but keep in mind that both partners will need supportive networks.

Recapturing Fantasy and Imagination After Trauma

In some ways, the problem of pornography use after trauma reflects a difficulty with recapturing fantasy after experiencing trauma. Psychologist and author Stephen Mitchell (2002) tells us that sexual relating is always partially an act of imagination. This is borne out by research that suggests that 70 percent of American men and women fantasize while making love (Fisher 2004). What it is they fantasize about is less important than their capacity to do so, because sexual desire, arousal, and orgasm are facilitated by the ability to trust and let go at the same time—to enter another state of consciousness.

In the aftermath of trauma, when safety and trust have been shaken, partners often lose the freedom to access the imagination, the fantasy necessary for sexual relating. We have seen that trauma often jeopardizes sexual relating because it has shattered illusions of safety, goodness, and ability to control life events. Life has become too painfully real, too frightening to relax one's guard. As Matt and Cathy found, fears of being known or of no longer knowing the other can make intimacy seem like too much of a risk. When trauma makes reality so frightening, some people desperately escape into pornography or promiscuity as a substitute for intimacy and connection with a partner.

Exercise: Recapturing Fantasy Together

Sharing fantasy is a tricky thing, because often the fuel of passion is the privacy of unshared thoughts that take you away from reality. However, you might consider sharing past or future fantasies as another way of moving beyond the realities of everyday life. Here are some ideas you might try:

- Write down a list of some places where you would like to make love with your partner sometime in the future. Talk about these places; fantasize about them.

- What was your fantasy after your first date with your partner? Take turns sharing your fantasies or writing them down.

- When do you fantasize most about having sex with your partner? Is it when you are in the car, listening to music, on a trip? Let him or her know.

- What would be your fantasy date if you were planning it for you and your partner? Write it down and share it.

- What fragrance invites the most fantasy for you? What fragrance sparks fantasy in your partner?

The Surprising Connection Between Separation and Intimacy

It may surprise you to know that psychological separation—the capacity to be alone and to understand the partner's capacity to be alone—fosters intimacy and actually improves sexual connection. It is the difference between needing to be with the other as opposed to wanting to be with the other that can change the quality of sexual exchange. For example, feeling that you have to be together to ensure love and commitment is different from looking forward to being with your partner because you love and enjoy him.

Strategy: Benefiting from Coming and Going

Following are a couple of strategies you can use to help you manage being separated from your partner and feed your relationship at the same time:

- Mutually supporting each other's enjoyment of friends, hobbies, and sports can actually enhance sexual desire. Comfortably spending time both in and away from the relationship—so that he has no problem with her nights at the gym and she has no problem with his weekend softball league—fosters the wish to return to the partner. It changes the pattern of relating. Each partner's outside activities enrich the couple's relationship and offer a view of the other from afar and through the eyes of other people.

- Couples often report that, when they are apart from their partner during the course of the day, they think more positively and romantically about them than at any other time. If we recognize the power of imagination in loving then we understand that it is our version of our partner that we are most in love with. This does not mean we don't want our actual partner with us. It just means the ability to be separate is a healthy and normal thing. You can't fantasize about someone who is always with you. Neurochemistry supports this idea—separation actually revs up dopamine and epinephrine, the hormones associated with sexual desire (Fisher 2004).

Embracing What Is New

One of the traps in the aftermath of trauma is the fear of who our partner has become. This fear is often masked by anger, disinterest, or avoidance. It's common for couples to hold onto an unspoken requirement that "everyone needs to stay the same" for the intimacy to resume—although, of course, this is impossible. Certainly, safety and trust are needed in order for partners to be intimate, but safety and trust are not incompatible with change and difference. In fact, in matters of sex, what is new and different may actually help recapture or expand intimacy, because it actually enhances desire.

Psychologists such as Stephen Mitchell (2002) and Esther Perel (2003), who address the loss of romance and sexual interest between partners, point to what happens when you know or think you know your partner so well—connection becomes predictable and sexual desire is diminished or put on the back burner. To keep things fresh and interesting, couples need to be familiar enough with each other to feel safe, and safe enough to accept (and even welcome) changes and differences in themselves and their partner.

Reclaiming and Renewing Your Sexual Relationship

It takes more than just showing up to create a good sexual relationship. It takes a plan—in this case, a plan to reclaim and renew the sexual connection you're missing in your relationship. You will find that making a plan to reconnect in this way can be sexually exciting. The anticipation, the pictures in your head, thinking about the way it is going to be—these all add to the erotic expectation and quite possibly the sexual connection. Regardless of the obstacles, when two people make a plan and share a goal to connect, it usually happens.

Make Room for Your Relationship

Start your plan to reconnect by acknowledging together that you want to make more room for your relationship in your lives. The first step is to evaluate your situation. Consider what, apart from yourselves, is getting in the way of your love life together. Think about this question independently and then make a combined list of the things that come to mind. For example, is there a lack of privacy in the physical layout of your environment? Are the children's schedules your only focus? Are you dealing with extended family demands, work schedules, or household chores that are unrealistic or conflicting? Are you both sleep deprived or exhausted? Once you identify some outside factors that may be interfering, consider addressing just one of these things at first, like adding a lock on your bedroom door, or rethinking the children's morning or evening schedules so you have a little more time together. If you look with an open mind, you might see something that can be shifted a bit to make living and loving easier.

Make the Time

We live in a culture where people have no time to spare and therefore must sometimes be reminded to make time for their intimate relationships. Over the years of couples living together, and even more so when lives have been disrupted by physical distance, illness, or tragedy, spending time together is often the first thing to go. Remember when you first met? At that time your focus was probably aimed at finding time to be together and thinking of new ways to enhance aspects of that time. If you had a preconceived expectation, it was probably a positive one, and maybe a sexual one. Even after all this time, you can focus on finding time for each other again.

Carving out time to find each other sexually begins with spending private time as a couple. Set aside twenty minutes just to make a plan to simply spend time together. Decide whether you would like to go out together or find a way to have some alone time at home. Divide up the tasks that will be necessary to make it happen—one of you can find someone to watch the kids while the other makes a reservation or plans the dinner at home. Put it on the calendar. Treat it as a sacred commitment that you both agree you will not break. Once you have done this, talk about creating a realistic plan to have more alone time in your lives. The more you do it, the more desirable and important it will become.

Practice Being Partners

Once you get in the habit of finding time to be alone together, be creative in the things you plan to do. Companions and confidants often become lovers. Shared experience, be it dinner, a movie, or a walk in the park, can begin to rebuild trust and connection and open the possibility of increased intimacy. When you return home from time you have enjoyed together, don't go back to the laundry, the computer, or the chores right away. Leave them for a little longer in favor of continuing the connection you have been enjoying. Notice how you are feeling. Is it possible to share your feelings either in words or actions? If you feel sexual, can you say that? If you would just like to hold your partner, can you tell him or her?

Set the Mood for Being Lovers Anywhere

Have an affair—with your partner! Turn the volume up on the relationship. Make stolen moments count. Take nothing for granted. Start leaving romantic or sexy phone messages on her private cell phone. Put a note on his car. Have a quick cup of coffee in the middle of your work day. Notice what the other is wearing. Steal a kiss in a public place. Make physical contact, even if you only rub your partner's foot under the table. Send a suggestive e-mail or text message.

Use Your Imagination

Select the day, the time, the location. Think about how you will invite your partner to join you, and enjoy the anticipation. Feel free to draw upon illusion and fantasy, because fantasizing about something that is arousing to you makes you a better partner. You'll know it works if the result is something pleasurable to you and your partner.

Watch a sexually arousing movie alone or together, or put on your favorite romantic song and visualize the most erotic sexual experience you have had (or long to have). Remember the compliments your partner gave you when you first met—replay them and add them to that scene in your mind. Remember a time your partner made you feel special, and visualize that scene, adding a sexual ending and enjoying the tenderness and feeling of being cared about.

Make Intimate Plans as a Couple

The most important things in sexual intimacy are mutuality and respect. If you both think that skinny-dipping in the neighbor's pool is a turn-on (and you won't upset your neighbor or get arrested), go for it. If only one of you likes this idea, then it won't work—but maybe a private shower together will. If you would like her to wear lingerie that she's not comfortable in, then it can't work. But if she wants you to wear skimpy underwear and you agree, then that's great. Maybe you can both choose something to wear that you like and think your partner will enjoy seeing you in. Remember, the most valuable factor in enhancing desire is the memory of a satisfying mutual experience.

Be Aware of Each Other's Needs

Be sure to support your partner to get what he or she might need to make sexual connection desirable. If desire, performance, or satisfaction is being affected by pain, erectile dysfunction, premature ejaculation, problems with lubrication, contraception, side effects from medication, or self-expectations to perform or have an orgasm, work as a team to solve the problem. Be patient, understanding, and collaborative. Go slowly, but seek professional help (from a urologist, gynecologist, pharmacist, psychologist, psychiatrist, or other expert) if needed. Try changing the setting, experimenting together, hitting the road, taking a break to play cards—anything that might help in a reassuring and supportive way—but don't give up.

Saying No and Hearing No

Worrying about whether your partner will reject you or you will upset your partner is like watching your feet while you are dancing—it's not great. Don't get trapped by preconditions and control issues. Allow choice. Both of you need to be able to say no so you can feel the true desire to say yes. When you say no, do it in a tender and intimate way; it is helpful to be loving and reassuring even as you decline. Too often, partners pair their "No" with a movement away from the other for fear of being misread or cajoled. Try to feel entitled but loving when saying no. For example, one way to make it clear you're not ready for sex but don't want to reject your partner is to kiss or hug your partner and say, "I'm sorry, I'm just not in the mood right now." Another possibility is to compliment the way your partner looks before saying, "I am exhausted, but I definitely want a rain check on being with you!"

Upon receiving a "No," some partners feel immediately rejected, put off, embarrassed, and angry. Again, you want your partner to choose to be with you, not comply out of fear or pressure. In a relationship, the safer it is to say no, the safer it is to say yes." Don't stop connecting because your partner can't or doesn't feel sexual. Instead let your partner know about your desire for him or her and that you accept your partner's choice. If one partner has a pattern of always saying no, then it is worth sharing your desire and wish to be sexual and your interest in knowing how your partner is feeling (see Guidelines to Enhance Intimate Communication earlier in this chapter).

Stay Positive as You Plan and Practice

Don't predict that your plan and your attempts to be intimate won't work. Negative predictions stop the momentum and rule out the possibility of learning something new together. If your plan to create a romantic sexual experience doesn't work the first few times, don't get discouraged. Could you learn the tango in one night?

Apply this positive attitude to any communications you have while engaged in a romantic moment. Remember you are trying to make love; conversation has its place, but be careful not to talk your partner out of the sexual moment or overlook the romantic power of silence. Being together in the dark, whispering, and using touch and body contact to communicate can be far more powerful than words. Eye contact is also powerful. It carries the intimacy well past the moment and into the other parts of your life. The meaningful look between you when both of you think something is funny, or the moment when you lock eyes across a room knowing just what the other is thinking—these are precious to your relationship. They are part of the fabric of your connection and can be called upon to ignite romance and increased intimacy.

When you and your partner do connect sexually or you have even the beginning of some shared intimacy, capture and hold on to the moment. That night or the next day, in an unexpected phone call or e-mail, let your partner know that you were with someone wonderful the night before. Keep it between you and keep it in mind. Keep the romance going.

Trust Yourselves to know When Professional Help Is Necessary

If you have been trying some of the strategies offered throughout this chapter but have not been successful in reestablishing the sexual intimacy you desire, you may find that professional help will add to your success. (See chapters 2 and 3 for tips on finding professional help.) Some couples need the safety, listening ear, and guidance of a skilled professional who can offer helpful interventions. Just walking into someone's office together for the first time is a mutual step toward desired intimacy.

Summary

In this chapter we have invited and guided you to reclaim your sexual intimacy and connection as sexual partners. We have underscored the inevitable impact of both sexual and nonsexual trauma on the relationship and sexual functioning experienced by many couples. We have made it clear that the common reactions and symptoms of hyperarousal, intrusion, numbing, and avoidance, by their very nature, compromise the safe, shared, relaxed space needed for sexual trust and enjoyment. When life has become too frightening and painfully real as a result of rape, combat trauma, or traumatic loss, it takes both time and small incremental steps to once again dance in the dark together. Recognizing this, we have offered guidelines and strategies for remembering who you once were, dealing with what has occurred, and renewing your intimate connection as lovers and partners. Drawing upon this renewed connection, in the next chapter you will work on finding a place for the traces of trauma in the life story you share.

5

Memories, Dreams, and Secrets: Finding a Place for Trauma

The action of telling the story in the safety of a protected relationship can actually produce a change in the abnormal processing of the traumatic memory.

—Judith Herman (1997)

The sunlight on a certain day, the screech of a car braking, even the smell of certain foods can trigger emotions that belong to another place and time. Images of people and places intrude into your memory; nightmares frighten both of you and disrupt sleep; once-treasured aspects of life are now avoided; secrets find a place between you. These are the traces of trauma. Confusing and disruptive, they make you doubt yourself and sometimes even fear your partner. Why do they persist? Where do you put them? How do you integrate trauma into your life?

The goal of this chapter is to find a place for your trauma in your sense of self, your relationship, and your world, which have been disrupted for the trauma you have faced. If one or both of you have experienced trauma then you have experienced the bewildering phenomenon that trauma disrupts both the ability to remember and the ability to forget. At times trauma intrudes in the form of memories, dreams, nightmares, and flashbacks such that you can't forget. At other times it leaves blanks, confusion, time lapses, and numbing, such that you can't remember.

This back-and-forth between knowing and not knowing is not only a reflection of the body and mind's lingering self-protection in the aftermath of danger but also is part of the journey toward recovery. In some ways finding a place for trauma involves looking back and looking forward in a safe way, in your own time, as you keep on walking.

As we have discussed, it is likely that your relationship has at times been intruded upon or strained by the knowing and not knowing that come with trauma. We will try to demystify these traces of trauma. The more you understand them, the more mastery you will feel over what is often frustrating and frightening. As you work together to try out new strategies for looking back and looking forward as a couple, you will find a place for your trauma.

Memories: Too Much to Remember, Too Painful to Forget

Memory is our ability to store, retain, and later recall information, experiences, and procedures. When working properly, memory is something most of us give little thought and attention to. If something slips our mind and we are unable to recall it, we know we can let it go and chances are it will soon come to mind. If it doesn't, we may return to the spot where we first had the thought, in the hope that it may jog our memory. Some people pride themselves on having an excellent memory; the rest of us make lists and take notes.

Without noticing it, we all draw upon different types of memory. We use sensory memory when we know that what we smell is pizza. We depend upon our working memory to keep information in the forefront of our minds as we write a report for work or follow the commands set out for a mission. We have short-term memory that allows us to remember the song we just heard on the radio or the football game we just watched, and long-term memory for material we studied in grade school or for the name of the family who lived next door when we were children. In fact, long-term memory is where most information is stored for later retrieval.

Long-term memory is not located in any one specific area of the brain; rather, information passes from short-term memory through the hippocampus in the brain and is stored in various places in the cortex. It is for this reason that damage to one part of the brain may lead to partial memory loss. You may have heard, or may know from personal experience, that age has a differential impact on memory—so seniors may have a difficult time with their memory of recent events but retain their memories of early days and childhood events.

Memory is a complex function of the brain, which researchers are learning more about every day. There are two main memory systems: declarative or explicit memory, which involves our conscious awareness of facts and events that have happened to us, and nondeclarative or implicit memory, which involves our memory of skills, habits, and reflexive actions such as riding a bike or driving.

Memory involves three stages: *encoding*, or processing information received by the brain, *storing it*, or making a permanent record of this information in various parts of the brain, and *retrieving it*, or recalling previously stored information in response to some stimulus or cue. Sometimes you might not know where you put the car keys because, as you were rushing around, you didn't really encode the location you placed them—in other words, as you were putting them down you were thinking about grabbing the kids' lunches, answering the phone, or feeding the cat. You didn't forget where you put them—you simply never encoded and stored the information.

Memory and Emotion

Emotion acts on all stages of memory—encoding, storage, and recall. We remember highly emotional positive and negative events more vividly than we remember what we ate for breakfast last weekend. The amount of emotion associated with an event affects our ability to remember it. The more emotional the event, either positive or negative, the more likely it is to be remembered.

At the time of an emotional event, information from your five senses enters your central nervous system, and the thalamus passes the information to the amygdala, the emotional processing center, or smoke detector, of your brain. The amygdala evaluates the information and passes it on to the other parts of the brain, including the hippocampus, for categorization and integration with preexisting information. The more significance the amygdala gives the information, the more closely the information will be attended to. However, when a traumatic event happens, this smoke detector goes off with such intensity that it registers danger in the body and prevents the categorization of feelings and sensations. In other words, when a situation is too emotional and the arousal of the amygdala is too high, the details of the event will not be organized or integrated properly. As a result, traumatic memories will not be fit into your existing schemas. They will be encoded as isolated images, sensations, smells, and sounds that don't fit anywhere into your existing story.

Memory Differences

We know that our memory of an event can be quite different from someone else's memory of the same event. What we remember of an event is based on who we are and what significance the event has for us. We also know that, just as there are differences in the ways men and women typically handle emotions, there are differences in the ways men and women process emotional memories. Shirley McPherson-Sexton (2006) found that men and women actually use different parts of the brain to encode emotional material. She also found that women have greater recall of emotional material but are more likely to forget information presented immediately before an emotional surge. This may explain why you and your partner remember different things about the traumatic experience you may have endured together. Consider Barry and Linda, struggling to recover from a car accident they were involved in three months before.

> *Barry was driving that night; the road was wet and curvy. When he swerved to avoid hitting a dog that had dashed into the road, the car fishtailed and hit an embankment, almost skidding off the road.*
>
> *Three months after the accident they had both recovered from their physical injuries, but the emotional injuries were slow to heal. Barry was replaying the accident in slow motion in his*

head. Although he felt guilty for losing control of the car, he also harbored a belief that, were it not for the argument he and Linda had been having at the time, the accident would never have happened. Why did she have to bring up the issue of relocating while he was driving? She knew how upsetting it was to him. Worse still was the fact that Linda did not remember what they had been talking about before the crash. The only thing Linda ever said about it was that she couldn't understand how it had happened. She never saw a dog—was he sure? He was usually such a careful driver, so how could he have lost control of the car?

Understanding Traumatic Memory

Traumatic memory is different from ordinary memory. Most often it is choppy, disorganized, and nonsequential. When one is relaying such a memory to others, it is often difficult to explain and not easy for the listener to understand. In contrast, ordinary memory is narrative, explicit, and declarative. It tells a coherent story with a beginning, middle, and end. If you were asked to recall the story of the first time you met, or a particularly special vacation or date, chances are your retelling of that event would be narrative in style. This is typical of ordinary memory. When something happens we integrate it into our existing store of information. It becomes part of the ongoing story of our lives.

Studies of trauma survivors suggest that most experience troubling intrusive memories of the trauma in the days and weeks after the event occurs (van der Kolk and McFarlane 1996; van der Kolk and Fisler 1995; Shalev 1992). For some, intrusive memories abate over the course of time. Others experience such memories months and even years later. Often, traumatic memories come back as emotional or sensory states with little verbal representation. For example, on rainy nights, Barry would often flash on the image of that dog on the slippery road. Although we can choose to call forth ordinary memories, like our first day on the job, and may even adjust the words we use to describe it depending on our mood, traumatic memories don't change over time and are triggered by certain situations. For many New Yorkers, a bright, clear early-fall day brings to mind the morning of September 11, 2001. Some firefighters say that whenever they enter lower Manhattan they can still taste the dust that surrounded them while working at the recovery site. Similarly, despite being avid football fans, many Katrina survivors are still unable to enter the refurbished Superdome without experiencing flashbacks to the awful conditions there after the flood.

Traumatic Memories and Triggers

The anniversaries of traumatic events such as a child's death, car accident, fire, natural disaster, or major catastrophes like 9/11 or the attack on Pearl Harbor often bring with them a resurgence of pain, grief, regret, guilt, and other feelings. Memories stirred up by the anniversary of a traumatic event may be stored in feelings, sensations, and dreams. Sometimes people are not consciously aware of the meaning of the day until they are stirred by feelings of anxiety or sadness that remind them. As time passes, some people think about the event less and less on a conscious level. Others take control of the impact of the day by marking it with a ritual, a prayer, or a planned event.

Triggers of traumatic memories may be associated with any of the senses—something that you see, hear, smell, taste, or touch. Sometimes a certain feeling, like sadness, terror, or shock, can even serve as the trigger of a traumatic memory.

Triggers may be shared by many, as is the case in the aftermath of war or a disaster, but they often tend to be specific to the person who has suffered the trauma. Similarly, in couples, what is a trigger for one may have little emotional impact on the other.

Marilyn found that being around family and friends helped her to cope after losing their son in Iraq. She was very uncomfortable with being home alone, when everything seemed to remind her of her son. Dave, on the other hand, felt like he was walking on eggshells when he was away from home. He found it unbearable when family and friends would mention the war and discuss their political stance against it. Not only did it immediately bring back the horror of seeing the marines come to the door, it filled him with rage and sadness.

When traumatic memories are triggered by environmental cues at unwanted and inopportune moments, they perpetuate the feelings of helplessness that are so problematic in the aftermath of trauma. These reminders interfere with the normal fading or integration of painful memories over time. For example, on the anniversary of 9/11 the media, in their attempt to inform the public, inadvertently retraumatize many who were there or were personally affected by the attacks. You can see how unexpected exposure to images and reminders of a trauma trips the neurochemistry associated with the event and interferes with well-paced integration of memories.

With Marilyn and Dave, recognizing the nature of each other's triggers helped them experiment until they were able to discover strategies that fostered their recovery. They discovered, for example, that Dave felt more comfortable being with family or friends when there was an activity planned, like a movie or football game, since the activity served as a buffer from discussion. And, at Dave's suggestion, Marilyn agreed to risk leaving the safety of family and friends to attend a bereavement group for military parents and found that others also avoided being home alone with memories. Realizing she was not alone in having this reaction and hearing the suggestions of other parents helped her. Unexpectedly, the bereavement group also worked for Dave, who found he could relax more with those who had faced the same loss. He didn't have to explain the pain to them—they knew all about it.

Dealing with Traumatic Memories

According to Judith Herman, a noted traumatologist, "The action of telling the story in the safety of a protected relationship can actually produce a change in the abnormal processing of the traumatic memory" (Herman 1997, 175). She tells us that along with this change comes relief and a reduction of post-traumatic stress symptoms. Similarly, Bessel van der Kolk (1996b), who has worked extensively with trauma, has hypothesized that, because trauma memories are registered as sensations and images in nonverbal areas of the brain, overcoming them requires transforming them into personal narrative. This means that the ability to tell the story of the trauma without reliving it is an important part of your recovery.

In order to heal, the person who has experienced the trauma needs to repeat the fragmented trauma story in a safe place with a safe person, so that he or she can fill in the missing pieces, integrate memories, and gradually construct a coherent narrative. Your couple relationship can be that safe place. Sue Johnson, a therapist known for her work with couples following trauma, stresses that this is an important aspect of all trauma treatment: "When the survivor can gather fragmented images, body sensations and thoughts, put them together in a context, and create a story of helplessness survived, this evokes a sense of mastery." This feeling of mastery helps the individual and the couple gain a sense of control over the trauma (Johnson 2002, 33).

To Talk or Not to Talk. Your partner's need to talk about a trauma may not always coincide with your ability to hear it. Adam Phillips (2006) says that another definition of listening is the capacity to deal with the feelings stirred in you by what you have heard. As we have mentioned, restoring your relationship serves not only as a cushion for the impact of trauma when it first occurs but also as a container—a "safe place" for you to go when it is time to emotionally revisit the event, integrate it, and regain mastery of your life story.

In our work with couples, we have found that the question of how much, or whether, to talk about the traumatic event together is a complicated and individual matter. Often one or both partners have worries about sharing. If you endured the trauma alone, you may wish to protect your partner from hearing the horror you experienced. If you are a member of the military or uniformed services you may feel that your partner can't understand. You may find yourself thinking, "You can't know because you weren't there." On the other hand, you may fear that if your partner comes to know what happened, he or she may never be able to see you quite the same way again. This is a common fear in combat veterans, who at times have difficulty making sense of what they or others faced in the chaos of war.

If you are the victim of a crime or assault, you may feel damaged or changed forever in a way that you fear your partner will not understand. In contrast, if the trauma is one that you both have experienced, you may be concerned that talking about your memories will awaken something in your partner that he or she is not ready for. You may be concerned that, instead of sharing in order to be helpful to one another, you will each be overloaded by the combined weight of your memories.

These are all valid and common concerns. The fear of talking about memories, however, can often keep a partner from even broaching the subject, preventing a couple from finding a safe way of dealing with the trauma. We have heard partners say things like, "Being left out is worse than anything I could hear," "He says I can't really understand how it was over there, but I just want to listen to feel close to him," and "No matter what happened I just want her to trust me with her pain."

A discussion of your fears and concerns about sharing can be the most valuable first step toward sharing and listening to traumatic memories. Essentially it is an opportunity to let your partner know that you want to share but you are worried. It is the expression of the wish for the other to be a trusted confidant. If your partner expresses a fear of sharing feelings, listen to his or her concerns. Suggest that you start slowly. Some couples test the waters by sharing overall feelings rather than details. Other couples feel safer about sharing when they have a prearranged way of signaling the need to stop. Essentially you are setting up a safe place for sharing trauma memories. (See the next section for strategies to help you share your memories.)

Strategy: Choose Your Time and Place

If you and your partner choose to discuss your memories of the event, consider following these guidelines. Don't expect too much at once. Remember that this is a process.

■ We suggest that you begin by sharing the concerns you each have about discussing the trauma (for example, "I'm worried that if I talk about it I will be upset for the rest of the night," "I feel bad enough for both of us; I don't want to upset you," "If I start crying, I may never stop"). Listening to the concerns and reminding each other that you will take it step by step, stopping if you need to, and reminding each other that you are trying to use your relationship as a healing place—all this will help. Just agreeing that it is hard to begin is a good place to start.

- **Set some structure for your talks.** Decide together how and where to have this discussion. Is eye contact desirable or too threatening? Should you hold hands? Offer an arm around the shoulder? There are no right or wrong answers to these questions; what is important is that you can decide these things together.

    Don't do too much all at once. To help you define what is too much, you may actually want to make a plan that includes a short time frame. It need not be long. Begin slowly, and plan on talking for just ten or fifteen minutes. This will keep the intensity at a manageable level. Afterward, ask one another how this worked and then increase or decrease the length of your "sessions" accordingly. This time frame structure is an important aspect of creating safety and is used in professional counseling. At the same time, don't rush yourself or your partner, and don't be afraid of silence; give each other time to think and speak. And, as we mentioned in the last section, it's important to decide on a signal to indicate when you need to come up for air.

    We recommend that you agree to bring your discussion to a close by doing something nonthreatening together, such as listening to music, getting something to eat, offering an affectionate hug, or going for a walk. Transitioning together back to a more comfortable activity helps each of you recognize that you need not move away from the other in order to get away from the trauma talk—rather, the connection between you can continue in a more casual manner until you agree upon another opportunity to share memories.

- **Decide what to talk about.** We suggest that you take turns selecting an aspect of the event you want to discuss (for example, hearing your child's diagnosis or seeing the headlights of the oncoming car). Decide who will go first. As the speaker, tell your partner what seems fuzzy or troubling about the aspect you have chosen. Agree together that the listening partner will continue to actively listen and not offer his or her recollections of the event until directly asked. This will allow you, the speaker, to explore what you do recall, and it may permit new memory to emerge. When you feel ready, you may choose to ask your partner, "Is your memory of this different from mine?" Or you may feel you want to hold off and continue to recall this event at your own pace.

It is important for the listener to respect this wish and resist the understandable temptation to help fill in the blanks or correct the "distortions" that you see your partner struggling with. Instead of correcting them, try to notice these differences with interest. Listen for changes in your partner's memory over time.

As you each share your version of the trauma, you may find it interesting to ask each other, "What was the worst part for you?" Sharing this information can be a strong factor in strengthening your connection and contributing to your recovery. As healing occurs, both your and your partner's memories of the event will likely become more narrative and sequential, less choppy and disorganized. And, of course, because you are two different people, they may always be slightly different versions. Put together, they become the story of the trauma you shared.

Ruminating versus telling the story. It is important to distinguish between telling the story of trauma as a part of the healing process and ruminating about the trauma. Ruminating involves obsessive recycling of thoughts and memories regarding the trauma, or worrying about potential bad outcomes from situations that have unfolded from the trauma. Let's look at Liz's experience with ruminating:

> Liz could not get the accident out of her mind. She replayed the scene over and over again, though nothing ever changed. One minute she would be doing her work, and the next she would be back on the boat, seeing her sister swimming, and then glimpsing her go under. As she replayed the scene over and over again, sometimes her thoughts shifted to her nephews, now motherless. What would happen to them? Would they be okay? What should she do? These questions remained unanswered, but they invaded her thoughts and kept her anxious and worried much of the time.

Liz's mental anguish is an example of ruminating. It is different from the constructive rebuilding you do as a result of sharing your story. But when Liz told her husband Dave that she wanted to talk to him about the accident, that's when the healing process began.

Liz and Dave chose a time and agreed to talk for twenty minutes. The first time they talked, she just talked about the day on the boat before the accident. Dave had been there but was below when everything occurred. He listened and let Liz pace the conversation. The second time, Liz said she wanted to talk about what happened in the water. She described her sister jumping into the water and waving. Liz remembered watching her sister swim while she was reading a book on the deck. She began to realize that perhaps her sister had been in the water longer than she had previously realized. This information seemed helpful to Liz. The next time they talked, she went back to this idea and also asked Dave if he had any thoughts or memories. He remembered her sister saying earlier that she had not been feeling well. He did not know if this might be related to the accident. This triggered more memories for Liz. They continued talking, and some pieces began to fit together. Liz began to accept that she might never know some of what had happened. Now, when she worried about her nephews, she brought her worries to Dave as well. They began to talk about how they might help, what role they might play with each of the boys. Liz began to feel better, although she would continue to grieve for her sister.

Understanding and honoring your differences. As we have mentioned, you and your partner are different people, and your responses to the same traumatic event may also be different. Remember that having a different recollection of an event isn't the same as disagreeing, not listening, or not caring.

Lack of recall may reflect a failure to encode or store memories because your conscious attention was distracted from the event, or it may reflect a form of psychological protection that happens when a traumatic event is so threatening that memories of it are split off from one's consciousness. In any case, you can assume that you and your partner won't be in the same place at the same time regarding your memory of the trauma you shared. Each of you may have a different recall of parts of the event or remember the same event with different details.

When only one partner has experienced the direct impact of the trauma, as in the case of an accident, assault, or combat, couples sometimes tend to overlook the traumatic experience of the other partner, who likely has his or her own haunting version of the trauma in the form of recurring images, sensations, and memories. Awareness of and respect for differences in traumatic memories is crucial to healing as a couple.

It is important to consider that sharing your versions not only brings you to the other side of the traumatic event together, but it also offers the possibility of collaborating, like Liz and Dave did—using the differences in your memories to reconstruct a coherent and shared narrative.

Revisiting the Scene. For many people, an important way of moving beyond the trauma and the feeling of being out of touch with the rest of the world is to clarify what happened in a way that makes it real in space and time. Sometimes this involves returning to the place of the accident. For example, one couple went back to the hospital where he had spent so much time in rehab. Another woman needed to go with her partner to the place he had once lived, which was destroyed by fire, in order to experience and bear witness to his loss.

Getting to know what happened in space and time is a step toward reducing the numbing that comes with trauma. Bearing witness at a time when there is no danger, and especially in the company of a safe person, allows revisiting and remembering without the overwhelming feelings that made numbing necessary. It fosters recognition that the experience had a beginning and end—that life preceded it and life will follow it.

Do you want to revisit the scene of the trauma together? If so, plan carefully when you will go and how long you will stay. Help anticipate the reactions you both might have, and some strategies you can use to deal with them. For instance, in case you are overwhelmed by anxiety, you and your partner can use the double deep breathing technique suggested in chapter 4. Accept that you may have a wide range of feelings— you may cry or feel numb. Decide ahead of time that you can leave right away if either of you feels too upset to remain, and agree to make a plan to talk together about what this experience was like for you.

Dealing with Avoidance, Numbing, and Dissociation

It is often in response to being haunted by traumatic memories that people who have suffered a trauma begin to organize their lives in order to avoid triggers of trauma. For many, this avoidance is compounded by a generalized numbing of responsiveness and detachment from life activities, or a dissociation or lack of conscious awareness of the trauma. The problem with these responses is that they prevent the revisiting, transformation, and integration of traumatic images, sensations, and feelings into narrative memory.

Avoidance

The avoidance symptoms that frequently result from trauma can vary markedly. Avoidance can include staying away from thoughts or feelings associated with trauma; use of drugs or substances as a way of avoiding the memories of trauma; or an actual avoidance of people or places that are reminders of the trauma. Right after the trauma or disaster, some avoidance actually helps a person to calm down by letting them stay away from stimuli that trigger traumatic feelings and memories. However, it is important that the person eventually begins to deal with possible triggers. Total avoidance makes this goal impossible, as do alcohol and drugs. The good news is that regulating your exposure to people, places, and things associated with the trauma by using the safety and support of your relationship will reduce your avoidance and promote healing.

In couples, however, a tricky conflict can come up: sometimes one partner's need to avoid triggers may conflict with the other partner's need to revisit, mourn, or memorialize. Here's an example:

> After the death of their two-year-old son, Keith and Deirdre focused on getting back to work and moving to a new home, at Deirdre's request. Things seemed to be improving until Deirdre walked into their new home and found that Keith had unpacked the last of their cartons and put a picture of David right in the living room. Deirdre could not bear it. She became furious with Keith, threatening to end the marriage. Keith tried to reason with her, explaining how important it was for him to remember the happiness they had shared as a family and honor David's memory. For Deirdre, however, looking at the picture only brought back the horror of the last days of David's life and her extraordinary pain at the loss.

Looking back, the differences in how Keith and Deirdre were handling their reactions to the trauma and grief of losing David were evident early on—when Keith wanted to remain in their home and Deirdre wished to move so she could begin to heal. Deirdre's style was more avoidant than Keith's; therefore, exposure to the picture of David disrupted her attempts to avoid the desperate feelings connected with the loss of her child. Her angry reaction is also typical of people's responses to trauma and the way in which anger can be used to mask grief and loss. In the face of this reaction, Keith was put in a difficult position. He could appreciate Deirdre's pain, but unlike Deirdre, he found comfort and a start at healing in remembering the happiness of the past.

By stepping away from the conflict a bit, Keith and Deirdre were able to work on a way to respect each other's needs. Keith agreed to keep his treasured pictures in his study, a room Deirdre rarely went into, and in his wallet. Deirdre agreed to listen to Keith when he needed to talk about David and to occasionally look at a photo. She told Keith she hoped it would not be too long before she could tolerate having the pictures displayed in the house. This meant a lot to Keith, who was beginning to fear that he was giving up too much and that together they were not going to be able to face and mourn this tragic loss. Now he had reason to believe this might change.

Numbing and Dissociation

Numbing, which is somewhat different from avoidance, is actually an extreme survival technique. In the face of life-threatening danger a person psychically closes off their feeling and awareness of some aspects of what they're experiencing as a way of not being completely overwhelmed.

Dissociation, in which the person enters an altered state of consciousness in order to escape an unbearable situation, is central to the numbing and constriction that follow from trauma. Theorists describe dissociation on a continuum, from mild to severe. You might experience a mild dissociative state when you're so caught up in thinking about something else that you miss your exit on the highway, while a severe dissociative state in the face of trauma can include the feeling that time has stopped, the feeling of being out of one's body, disorientation, or tunnel vision (Herman 1997; Henry 2004). Some say it is the escape when there is no escape. During a traumatic experience a person has a splitting of consciousness. Essentially, dissociation allows a person to observe the event from an emotional distance, like a spectator—protected from having an awareness of what has actually happened. Although dissociation serves as a protection at the time of the trauma, it results in the lack of integration of traumatic memories (van der Kolk 1996b).

More specifically, those who experience some type of dissociation often have a residual numbing that affects the quality of their life in all dimensions. They may have a lack of emotional reactivity, less interest in things they used to enjoy, and a sense of detachment and foreshortened future. First responders and military personnel in particular may experience these symptoms, since their work necessitates a "functional numbing" so they can regulate anxiety and stay focused on the mission. The problem is that when you stop feeling danger and dread, you also stop feeling vital and connected.

The tragic aspect of numbing is that it affects not only the connection with one's spouse or partner but also the connection in other close relationships. Research has shown that avoidance and numbing symptoms of PTSD are highly correlated with impaired parent-child relationships. Often the numbing, detachment, and avoidance that a veteran experiences makes it difficult for him to become involved in normal interactions with his family and children (Ruscio et al. 2002).

Reconnecting to Feelings

Gradually sharing the story of the trauma usually begins to ease symptoms of avoidance and numbing. Couples who start this journey with very different symptoms and coping strategies often find that sharing the story at their own pace helps them relate to one another and reconnect to their feelings.

Reconnecting to your own and other people's feelings will give you a sense of being more in control that facilitates recovery. One way to do this is to start by acknowledging or making note of feelings that are different from the painful ones. It is sometimes easier, for example, to begin to experience positive feelings in new or different places that have fewer reminders of the trauma.

Strategy: Finding Safe Opportunities to Reconnect with Feelings

- **Being anonymous.** We often hear people speak about practicing reconnection to their feelings by being with people who are unaware of their trauma. This can provide an opportunity of just being *themselves* back in the world, feeling *normal* in the presence of people who are not worried about them or watching for signs of the trauma to intrude. For some, volunteering to help others, such as coaching a Little League team or reading to the blind, provides the opportunity to have feelings and connect with people who are not aware of their trauma. For others, being in the world can involve finding a new activity or focus—like buying and caring for a pet together with their partner, or taking music lessons with one of their children.

- **Being part of a trauma group.** Sometimes the reverse is true—for some, it becomes enormously helpful to have the validation of feelings of others who know and have shared the same trauma. Talking about feelings from a safe distance can provide opportunity to begin to reconnect with one's own feelings. For example, in one program, groups of couples watched films and discussed the feelings they saw depicted in the films. At a safe distance, the opportunity to talk about someone else's feelings while sharing time with a partner and other couples can help people reconnect to their feelings in a safe, supportive environment. Consider hosting a movie night, either with just the two of you or with another couple, to provide yourselves with a similar opportunity.

Seeking Professional Help for Traumatic Memories

Sometimes a partner or couple will need the help of a professional to deal with intrusive memories. Therapy techniques like eye movement desensitization and reprocessing (EMDR) and prolonged exposure therapy (PE), which is a form of cognitive behavioral therapy (CBT), have been effective in reducing and integrating the intrusions of flashbacks, traumatic images, and sensations for people with traumatic memories. These techniques reactivate the trauma neurophysically in a safe environment created by either a therapist or a group. They allow the individual to retell memories in small steps while simultaneously using relaxation and other techniques that carefully control remembering and may lessen the traumatic nature of the memory and facilitate integration (van der Kolk, McFarlane, and van der Hart 1996). If you and your partner find that, despite trying many of our recommended strategies, one or both are suffering with the traumatic extremes of knowing (flashbacks and traumatic memories) or not knowing (dissociation, avoidance, and numbing) and it is jeopardizing your relationships at home and in the work world, then it is time to seek professional help. For military and veterans, the U.S. Department of Veterans Affairs and the Department of Defense provide clinical services using many of the techniques described in this section. For civilians as well as military and veterans, the websites for the National Center for Post-traumatic Stress Disorder and the American Psychological Association offer links to professionals who can work with the trauma symptoms as described here.

Night Shift: Dreams and Nightmares

Dreams and nightmares often play a significant role in trauma—both as symptoms and as sources of recovery. Though people's memories of their dreams and the attention they pay to their meaning and message vary greatly, after a trauma it is important and beneficial not only to attend to your dreams but to share them with your partner. The following information will help you to understand why this is important and then help you to begin to exchange this information safely and productively.

The Importance of Dreams

Research has shown that one of the reasons why we need to sleep is that we also need to dream. Experts used to believe that dreams served to protect sleep, but now the thinking is that sleep serves to preserve the capacity to dream. There seems to be a neurological need to dream—when you deprive people of rapid eye movement (REM) sleep, the part of the sleep cycle in which dreams occur, they compensate by having more dreams (Fossage 1997).

Researchers think that REM sleep and dreams play an integral role in helping us to regulate our emotions, consolidate memories, process information, and adapt to stress (Fossage 1997). It is therefore not surprising that dreams play a significant role in the processing of and recovery from trauma. In fact, according to James Fossage's organizing model of dreaming, dreams help integrate emotionally arousing events into preexisting structures within the memory system. Dreams foster development of new views of self, facilitate new learning, and aid problem solving. They also help us deal with emotionally laden material and integrate trauma. Consider the following dreams, for example:

> *A new mother, diagnosed with cancer, dreams that she enters a room where everyone is seated in a circle, and a chair left for her is empty. On it is a Jack-in-the-box toy that pops up with a card reading "cancer."*

The dream reveals the diagnosis's assault on this woman's definition of self and her unconscious connection between this horror and her awareness of being a new mother, represented by the toy.

> *A rape victim repeatedly dreams in fractured images of her attack. As she begins to face this trauma in counseling, her dreams begin to change. Increasingly, there are other people in the dream who help her. Eventually in her dreams she begins to confront the molester with the words "I'll take you down first."*

In her dreams, this young woman begins to protect herself and gets help. Her dreaming both reflects and adds to her movement out of helplessness.

The Benefits of Remembering Dreams

Dreaming is one way of developing, regulating, and restoring psychological functioning. Positive, negative, frightening, and neutral dreams are all in some way representing something you are working on or trying to integrate. In a dream, you may register a feeling of satisfaction, glimpse a more assertive self, experience a longing for a lost loved one, deal with a conflict, feel anger, or experience a terrifying replay of a traumatic event. Remembering dreams, writing them down, and trying to understand them all foster a sense of mastery, control, and self-understanding. In the case of trauma, working on dreams helps change traumatic fragments from isolated images and bodily sensations into narrative experience that can be integrated into life experiences.

Mark Blechner (1998) tells us that what is special about dreaming is that it allows us to have thoughts that can't be put into words. We have found, particularly in trauma work, that once people start remembering their dreams they start to be aware of their movement from pain to recovery as registered in their unconscious. They then follow a process of increasing self-awareness. They come to see that sometimes a dream may seem unclear, silly, or confusing, but that the next dream seems to clarify things more. They start to notice certain symbols or ways they represent feelings in dreams. One woman recovering from rape knew that she was registering anxiety whenever her little dog was lost or in danger in her dreams.

Exercise: Keeping a Dream Journal

A valuable way to use your unconscious to help you understand and integrate the trauma you have experienced is to keep a dream journal. Keep a book that you use only for this purpose at your bedside. (It is best that you and your partner keep separate journals. You will have the opportunity to share if you choose.) Each morning, write down the date and any dream that you can remember, even ones that are short and ones that are not specifically connected to the content of the trauma. If you can remember only an image, like a bird, a lamp, or a person, record it—later that day you may remember the dream that the image appeared in. Jot down any associations the dream brings up for you. You will likely begin to see common themes, symbols, and even recurrent dreams.

Don't let this exercise become work or cause for worry. Just use it as a way to follow the journey of your unconscious as you recover. You will read about more tips to enhance your understanding in the next section.

The Value of Sharing Dreams With Your Partner

In our work with couples, we have found that sharing dreams as a couple enhances the relationship in the following ways:

- It enhances intimacy, because as you try to understand each other's dreams you are invited into your partner's private thoughts and feelings.

- When partners have become isolated or distant from each other, a dream can become a point of reference that stimulates and fosters more sharing.

- Sharing positive dreams offers what many relationships need, a shared positive experience. For example, if a partner shares a dream in which he or she was able to fly and had a wonderful experience of moving at will and looking at the town below, the person's partner gets to share that sense of freedom, experience relief that the partner is feeling well, and partakes in the flight.

- Understanding and talking about positive and neutral dreams may lower anxiety and foster a dialogue for working together to detoxify nightmares, flashbacks, and other intrusive trauma symptoms. It may help partners trust each other in the process of seeking help for these common imprints of trauma.

* When dreams represent an attempt to deal with feelings of terror or vulnerability, then remembering dreams and sharing them with your partner will often move unconscious feelings into a place where you can start to consciously experience them. For instance, a police officer who had to deal with a child's drowning has dreams that he has lost his own baby in a store and can't find him. If he remembers his dream, it might offer him some conscious insight into his feelings around this critical incident at work. If he shared this dream with his spouse, their connection to each other could help him to understand and process the anguish and helplessness he felt in the face of a child's death.

Although everyone dreams, people have different capacities to connect with their dreams. Research suggests that people come out of REM sleep into a waking state differently. For some it is a smooth and quick transition from dream to waking state, making memory of dreams easier than it is for those who take longer to move from dream to waking state. The neurophysiology that affects such patterns may simply be different. The smoother the transition, the more the dream is remembered (Fossage 1997).

If you want to see if you can improve your dream recall, try one of several techniques, beginning with simply believing in your ability to recall your dreams. It is helpful, as suggested in the last exercise, to keep a pad and pencil near your bed so you can record any dream fragments as you wake, not only in the morning but also in the middle of the night. If possible, do not use an alarm for waking up in the morning, since this jarring reentry into wakefulness can disrupt your ability to recall your dreams. If you haven't been remembering your dreams since the trauma, this may be a protective mechanism; your dream recall will return as you become psychologically ready. Be patient with yourself—you are handling a lot right now. And dreams are not the only way to access and share your unconscious.

Sharing the Unconscious ... Even if You Don't Remember Dreams

The fact that you don't remember your dreams doesn't mean you cannot connect with your unconscious, nor does it reduce your chances to share valuable information with your partner. We encourage partners to share daydreams, associations to song lyrics and movie scenes, memories, flashbacks, written notes, and diary entries, because all of these are also part of the fabric of your unconscious. Here, too, you may find threads that connect to aspects of your traumatic experience that you are trying to work on. For example, you may find that your connection to a particular song lyric is now different than it was before, or you may find yourself recalling a particular film or book. In exploring this memory, you may discover its connection to your recent traumatic event or to a specific feeling you are dealing with, such as anxiety or grief. Discussing these things with your partner can be beneficial, as he or she may see this connection before you do. Don't be surprised if, as you do this, you begin to recall dream fragments that are related as well.

Exercise: Dream Collaboration

Dreams are valuable in their nature and function and can be used in a collaborative way by couples. Drawing upon James Fossage's organizational model of dreaming (1997), we consider the content of your dreams to be very important. The dreams' content, in the form of people, images, symbols, location, action, themes, and metaphors, reveal what you are thinking, feeling, and trying to process and restore. In dream work there are no right or wrong answers. The process of writing about, talking about, and sharing a window into your unconscious is far more important than finding answers.

When you are sharing your dreams with your partner, consider following these guidelines:

1. **Choose a dream to share with your partner.** You may want to start with a positive one, or one that seems easy to understand. Try to write it down right after you wake, even before you get out of bed.

No matter how sure people are that they will remember their dream, by the time they pick up their toothbrush, it is often gone.

2. **Read the dream to your partner and have him or her repeat the dream back to you.** Repeating your dream helps your partner to experience the dream and allows you to hear it at a distance. Invite your partner to think of the dream as if it belonged to him or her.

3. **Answer and discuss the following questions together:**

   * **What is the feeling of the dreamer in the dream?** This is an important question because, though the meaning of other aspects of the dream is up for interpretation, only the dreamer knows the feeling of the dream. What would your partner feel if it were his or her dream?

   * **Is this a feeling the dreamer can recognize in his or her present waking life?** Sometimes our dreams include feelings that are the same or completely different from ones we have been feeling during our waking hours. For example, if we hold back our feelings during the day, our rage or fear might get worked out in our dreams. Because partners share conscious and unconscious perceptions, it is valuable to hear if your partner has also been having this feeling.

4. **Consider the elements of the dream.** What is the setting of the dream? What is the narrative or storyline? What is the main character doing? What is happening to whom? Who are the people in the dream? Why are those particular people in this dream? Does it include someone from the past? What was your relationship with this person? Does the presence of this person represent certain feelings? Does this person represent a part of you? Is this person similar to you or to someone in your present life?

5. **Connect the dream with your present waking life.** Dreams are often colored by the details of everyday life, known as the *day residue*. For example, you are worrying about looking good for your job interview and you dream that you are wearing a suit with a fabric that looks unprofessional—it has the same design as the wallpaper you recently hung in your kitchen. Dreams most often reflect your attempt to register, work on, or integrate something in your life.

Consider whether your dream registers something about you, your partner, or someone else in your life. Does it reflect your mastery of a challenge, a conflict, or a fear? Could it reflect the imprint of trauma, the sadness and grief over a lost loved one, fear about not being safe, or a sense of power over what has been threatening?

6. **Sum up your observations by answering the question, "Why did I have this dream?"** Your answer may offer valuable insight, such as "I am still mourning my brother," "I am trying to get comfortable in this town," or "I'm frightened of never seeing my wife again, even though I'm home from Iraq and we are safe."

Understanding Nightmares

Disturbed dreaming is extremely common after trauma, and nightmares are the most frequent form of disturbed dreaming. Nightmares are so common, in fact, that their prevalence after trauma exposure is as high as 90 percent (Levin and Nielsen 2007). Nightmares are considered part of the process of reexperiencing unresolved trauma.

What is a nightmare? A nightmare is a frightening dream that usually awakens the person during REM sleep. It may replay the trauma, it may be similar to or different from the trauma, or it may interweave multiple traumas into the same dream—even including events that occurred several years apart. Nightmare sufferers often experience smells, sounds, and even physical pain in their dreams, some of which reflect severe emotional distress.

Nightmares can start immediately following exposure to a traumatic event, or their onset may be delayed for several years—triggered at times by another trauma. Common triggers of trauma dreams or nightmares include anniversaries of the initial traumatic event, sensory stimuli such as smells or sounds, and certain emotions that are associated with the original trauma. Often tension-producing life events and transitions can also activate nightmares. For example, when Gabe was suddenly let go from his job of twenty-five years, he began to have nightmares about the car accident that had killed his son.

It is normal for nightmares to come and go, and it is instructive to try to understand what event, feeling, or situation might have tripped a nightmare. For example, it was not until some Vietnam veterans saw news clips from the war in Iraq that feelings from their own earlier combat trauma were activated and emerged as nightmares.

Seeking Professional Help for Nightmares

Chronic nightmares can have a terrifying and disruptive impact on both the person having the nightmares and his or her partner, because they often resensitize and retraumatize both partners. We will next suggest certain strategies for couples to use to address nightmares, but in the case of chronic nightmares that continually impair sleep, create nighttime fears, reverse sleep patterns, and impair the person's ability to function during the day, it is important to seek professional help. A professional can assess the problem and make recommendations for therapy, medication, or both.

Strategy: Dealing with Nightmares

A number of professionals use and recommend techniques for working on dreams that alter aspects of the nightmares to defuse and change the emotional meaning of these dreams (Coalson 1995; Garfield 1995). Let's draw upon these techniques to consider ways in which you and your partner might deal with nightmares together. These are simply suggestions; use the steps below in a way that seems to work best for you and your partner.

1. **Share the nightmare.** If the dreamer has not written the nightmare down, the nondreamer partner can write down the dream as it is being shared. Try having the nondreamer repeat the nightmare back to the dreamer as if it were his or her own dream. This often allows for some distance, which helps to detoxify the nightmare.

2. **Give it a title.** Work together to create a new title for the nightmare, one that changes the association from negative to positive. The goal of this technique is to replace the frightening aspects of

a nightmare with a sense of confronting and conquering danger. For example, instead of referring to it as "my nightmare of being chased," you might call it "my superhero dream." Instead of being title "the dream where the baby falls," it could be called "the flying baby dream."

3. **Alter the storyline.** This technique changes the action of the story so that it has a positive theme and ending. For example, instead of seeing the oncoming car headed straight for your car, rewrite the dream so that you press a button and the car is lifted above the highway, coming to rest on a calm and beautiful beach. Next, think about and visualize the positive version of the nightmare. You want it to become a familiar image that is available to you whenever you are confronted with the vision of the oncoming car, whether you are sleeping or awake. You might set aside a few times a day to do this—perhaps when you are taking a walk, riding the train to work, walking the dog, and getting ready for bed. Sometimes sharing aloud with your partner invites him or her to join you in creating and elaborating on the new image, moving it to an even better place. Remember, you are choosing to transform your dream experience. You may feel some initial discomfort. Take your time. If this technique feels very burdensome or upsetting, put it aside. You can always try again a different day or a different way.

4. **Empower yourself.** One of the ways to undo the feeling of terrifying reality in nightmares is to prepare a positive statement in your mind before going to sleep. For instance, Bob Coalson (1995) gives the example of a young soldier who prepared himself for frightening recurring dream of facing an enemy by telling himself before going to sleep, "This is my dream. It is my creation. It does not have to frighten me."

Reconnecting Beyond Your Secrets

You may have heard the expression "You are as sick as the secrets you keep." From a couple's perspective, we would change that to read, "You are as separate as the secrets you keep." In the aftermath of trauma, the impact of secrets on a couple can be devastating. Secrets lock one partner in with pain and keep one partner out. Most often they create a distance that makes intimacy and closeness very difficult.

There are many reasons why people keep secrets in the aftermath of trauma. Often the subject of the secret is associated with negative self-judgment, guilt, and fear of hurting others or being hurt. A common cause is the actual experience of intrusive symptoms. Embarrassed by the nightmares, flashbacks, difficulty concentrating, or inability to feel, the partner having these symptoms often keeps them a secret, fearing that he or she is crazy, damaged, undesirable, or a burden to the family. As a result, the person avoids contact or intimacy with others in order to hide the secret.

Sometimes the secret is driven by the hidden need to remain loyal to another who has died, or by feelings of guilt over not having prevented a loved one's death or harm. Sometimes, often in the aftermath of combat, a soldier bears the secret fear that his or her life was bought at the cost of a friend's death, a confused fear that interrupts mourning, healing, and connecting.

In addition to having to cope with these difficult secrets, the traumatized person may also believe that sharing what he or she is hiding would harm the partner or the relationship. The nontraumatized partner may feel relieved, preferring not to know, or more frightened, wishing to know what's going on. Sometimes, in the absence of information, the nontraumatized partner creates his or her own images that are as bad as or even worse than what the traumatized partner is hiding.

No matter what their reasons or causes may be, secrets never protect relationships. Rather, they add a feeling of disconnection or loss, as one partner struggles to understand without having access to all pieces of the puzzle.

Safe Sharing

In our work, we have found that often, when people do not want to expose their partners to the horrific events they have witnessed, they are unable to talk about the experience at all. But we have discovered a way out of this dilemma: sharing the *feelings* about the traumatic experience without sharing all the details.

Strategy: Safe Sharing and Listening

How to share one's feelings and not the related details may not be clear right away. Most people do not separate what they saw or did from what they felt at the time or what they are going through in the present. But it can be done. For instance, a combat vet who served as a medic tells his wife, "I felt more helpless than frightened when I was trying to save those kids." An accident victim says, "I still can't get over the feeling of being outside myself—like someone else was crashing into that truck." A rescue worker who helped in the aftermath of Hurricane Katrina says, "You would not have wanted to be there. It was awful—the images keep me awake. I wish I could forget. And I wish I could have done more." In the face of haunting memories, articulating a general sense of the traumatic experience and the feelings connected with it can help you stay safely connected to your partner.

The nontraumatized partner can do a lot to help make this strategy effective. First, let your partner know that you are interested and available to listen to whatever he or she is able to tell you. Let your partner know directly that you do not need to hear the details; rather, encourage your partner to describe how he or she is feeling. You may have read that telling the story is an important part of trauma recovery, but do not push for the story if your partner isn't comfortable telling it. Conversations like this need not last more than a few moments to promote connection and help both of you feel less alone. In addition, your compassionate presence and encouragement will be of great benefit to both of you.

Finding a Place for the Secrets of Trauma and Moving On

As you can see, fears and negative self-judgment often turn into secrets that we carry and find difficult to share. We know from the work of James Pennebaker (Pennebaker, Kiecolt-Glaser, and Glaser 1988) and many others who replicated his study that when people are asked to write about their traumatic experiences for twenty to thirty minutes a day for a six-week period, their mood, functioning, and physical and emotional stress levels improve. Karen Skerrett (2003) draws upon storytelling as a way to empower the "we" feeling and promote healing in couples when one is facing serious illness. Skerrett reminds us that the story about ourselves that we perpetually update—both to ourselves and others—is a way in which we make meaning of the events that happen in our life.

To help make meaning of the traumatic event you have faced, try writing the story of that trauma. Writing a narrative of the trauma can provide a safe way to revisit, share, and integrate your story and the secrets it contains. Write each day for a set period of time, rather than sitting down and writing for a long time. This will give you more opportunity to slowly build on the necessary details of the story and to experience the courage you need in order to bear witness to what has happened.

Exercise: Writing a Narrative of the Trauma

Over the course of four to six weeks, aim to write the story of the traumatic event(s) you have experienced—in other words, what happened, who was involved, and what your thoughts, feelings, and reactions were. Write about the aftermath as well. Include if you can any secrets that have burdened you. You will find that just writing your story will trigger memories. Take your time and write for no more than twenty to thirty minutes at a time. If you feel overwhelmed, remind yourself that you are in charge; stop and take a break if you need to—you can always go back to it the next day.

If you're wondering how to begin, try starting at the end and working backward. Or you can write the big events first and then add details.

Remember that secrets are symptoms of fear that become heavy baggage because they never get shared. By sharing them in a story, you are relieving yourself of the burden of carrying all that heavy baggage.

Here are a few guidelines for writing and sharing your story:

1. To begin, each of you should have a new notebook in which you can separately write about the trauma or your version of the traumatic event(s) and aftermath for twenty to thirty minutes every day. If you prefer, you can do your writing on your computer in a secure file. Just remember to make a backup copy of the file—this is not something you would want to lose. Even if only one of you was directly involved in the trauma, it's okay for both partners to write the story—the partner who didn't go through the crisis event has also had a significant experience that needs to be witnessed.

2. Decide whether you want to write at the same time in different rooms, side by side, at separate times, and so on.

3. After two weeks, decide whether you want to share some part of what you have written with your partner, perhaps a section, a memory, or a paragraph. Sharing will likely strengthen your trust and connection with each other. Choose a time when you will be relaxed, unhurried, and uninterrupted. Exert no pressure on each other, and support each other's efforts.

4. Decide whether you will continue to share sections or wait to hear the entire story. When the time comes, think about whether you want to exchange notebooks or if you will read aloud to one another. Either of these methods is fine, as long as both of you agree.

5. If you will be reading one another's writing silently you can do this at the same time. Don't make verbal comments while reading, and do not interrupt one another. It may be helpful to have a pad and pencil nearby in case there is something particular you want to remember and comment upon later. Don't mark your partner's work; keep your own notes separately.

6. If you will be reading out loud to one another you will need to decide who will read first. In choosing this method you may want to set aside two separate times for this activity, since it may be too

much to read and comment on in one sitting. Listen quietly and attentively as your partner reads.

7. Whichever method you use, decide if you just want to listen and let some time pass to process the other's story, or whether you want to comment. If you decide you want to comment, start by sharing your feelings when hearing your partner's material. Comment on aspects of the writing that were particularly striking to you. Mention aspects you would like to hear more about. Express your appreciation to each other for this shared experience.

8. Now that you have written and shared your separate stories of the trauma, you have the possibility of the very interesting and rewarding experience of writing your joint story—who you were before, what happened, the journey you faced, how you coped, and where you ended up. If you decide to try this, set aside time for joint writing, and take turns writing or talking and transcribing. Figuring out how you will write your story is a part of your story.

Summary

Finding a place for trauma is a complicated but necessary step in recovery. Traumatic events trap us in the paradox of knowing and not knowing. Their imprints in the form of memories, sensitivity to triggers, dreams, or nightmares stay with us because they are difficult to assimilate into who we were and the lives we once knew. Recovery involves remembering what happened and mourning what has changed and been lost. It involves finding a way to adapt to what is different by expanding your sense of self and the life you share together. In this chapter you have worked on doing this. If you have followed some of the strategies, you have told your story, shared dreams, and perhaps found a safe way to reveal secrets. Your goal has been to use your relationship to find a place for trauma so that it will not dominate your everyday existence or steal your future. In the next chapter you are going to draw upon your resiliency as individuals and as a couple to make new memories as you move together into the future.

6

Healing Together: Enhancing Couple Resilience

The properties linked to resilience lie in the "we," not the "I,"
and arise through the process of connecting.

—Samuel Shem and Janet Surrey (1998)

You have now gained a greater understanding of what trauma is and how it has affected your relationship. However, the question remains: "How do you move into the future together as a couple?" Earlier strategies have been designed to help you talk and listen to each other about the trauma you have faced, to handle anger, to reclaim intimacy, and to find a place for the imprint of trauma in your life and relationship. The goal of this chapter is to reinforce and enhance your resilience as a couple so that you can move into that future.

Definitions of Resilience

Resilience can be understood in a number of ways. The most common definition of *resilience* is the capacity to adapt in the face of adversity—essentially the ability to bounce back from traumatic and difficult life events. Resilience can be considered a function of individual traits such as physical strength, intelligence, interpersonal strengths, independence, sense of humor, creativity, and spirituality. In addition, resilience is also demonstrated in social skills, problem-solving skills, regulation of self-esteem, utilizing positive emotions, and the existence of strong family, work, or community networks (Norman 2000). Although some theorists (Bonanno 2004) consider resiliency to mean the ability to maintain a stable equilibrium in the face of aversive life circumstances, we have seen that it is often impossible to maintain stability or the status quo in the aftermath of trauma, disaster, or war. We agree with those who see recovery as an example of resilience because it emphasizes the capacity to find a way back to successful adaptation and functioning even after a period of disorganization and disruption (Roisman 2005). We also embrace the view of resilience as a set of dynamic processes that can evolve and expand over time (Van Vliet 2008; Wilkes 2002). In this light, we will invite you to consider your post-traumatic growth (PTG)—the growth that trauma survivors often experience in life awareness and functioning (Tedeschi, Park, and Calhoun 1998).

Factors of Resilience

Let's look at the factors and capacities that have been associated with individual resiliency, and adapt them to you as a couple (Van Vliet 2008; Maddi 2002; Norman 2000; Tedeschi and Kilmer 2005). As you consider these, you will likely notice that they inevitably overlap. For example, partners who consider themselves capable of handling adversity most probably value each other's resiliency traits and know how to solve problems collaboratively. Couples who maintain a positive outlook usually know how to put things in perspective, handle differences, apologize, and forgive.

Each of the following sections addresses one or more of the factors and capabilities associated with resiliency. With each, you will recognize qualities that already define your resiliency as a couple and also those that you can use to enhance it. You may find aspects of your relationship that you have taken in stride and not noted as a source of resilience. You may notice others that have changed in one direction or another as you have worked your way through the trauma. All of these are worth considering as you think together about what it means to be resilient as a couple.

Hardiness

Similar to resilience, hardiness is thought to be essential not only for surviving trauma or disaster but also for thriving under stress (Maddi 2002). Three key characteristics are associated with hardiness and are identified in people who have turned adversity to their advantage: commitment, control, and challenge. You may recall the section on anger management for couples in chapter 3, where we underscored that partners are more effective in managing anger when they have a mutual commitment to respect and protect each other from destructive anger; they use preventive steps and communication to control the escalation of anger; and they take on the challenge of couple anger management. You can imagine how such characteristics will expand couple resiliency in other areas.

Commitment

In a relationship between two people who may be reeling after a trauma, a commitment means that they are taking an active and involved role in addressing the situation they are facing. It also implies a commitment to each other during the recovery from trauma—an understanding that no matter how rough it gets, the other will be there. You intend to face adversity together, with a strong commitment to one another and the future.

Control

The hardy couple strives to influence outcome rather than taking a passive position or feeling powerless. Each believes that it is possible to have control of at least some aspect of events, even terrible ones. However, it's important to be able to identify what can and what cannot be controlled—and use one's energy in an effective way. Not only can the partners help each other recognize and accept what can and cannot be controlled, but they can also support and encourage each other to take a proactive position. Often, they take turns holding out hope or optimism in a way that allows them both to keep trying.

Perhaps you have been diagnosed with a serious illness. Initially it is difficult to accept the accuracy of the diagnosis, and you may spend time and energy on denial or wishing it were not so. When you are able to face it as a couple, you begin to focus on what can be changed, rather than worrying about something that is out of your control. You begin to educate yourself about available options and engage in a problem-solving process that will allow you to decide on a course of action. As a couple, you support one another by taking turns so that each of you has an opportunity to express the feelings of sadness and fear while the other continues the research and planning necessary to stay on course. The one thing you know you can control is that you are going to face the illness together.

Challenge

The ability to see trauma or adversity as a challenge that, when overcome, offers enhancement and growth is a powerful factor of couple hardiness. It is the ability to reframe the situation, so that you experience stressful situations as opportunities.

For example, on your return from military service, you and your partner may be facing the challenges of readjustment to civilian and family life together. It is important for you to recognize that you have already overcome enormous challenges and demonstrated resiliency as you hung together so many miles apart. One of you managed alone with home life, bills, and babies, while the other faced the unimaginable demands of war. While you face new challenges, you probably have inner resources you never imagined you had.

Positive Outlook

Resiliency is connected with the ability to feel positive emotions and maintain a positive outlook. Research suggests that resilient people don't just feel positive; they draw upon positive coping strategies like benefit finding, positive reappraisal, humor, and infusing ordinary events with positive meaning to deal with stress (Ong et al. 2006).

A couple who can draw upon the positive outlook and positive coping strategies of one or both partners will have more resiliency in dealing with and recovering from traumatic life events. Rather than focusing on regrets, catastrophizing, blaming, and self-blaming, resilient couples assess the bigger picture, remain optimistic, and seek to find the lighter moments, even the benefits, in adversity. They exhibit curiosity about change and have positive expectations about the outcome of change. They rarely lose sight of their strengths both as individuals and as a couple. They prioritize well, each reminding the other not to "sweat the small stuff." They convey hope to one another and can hold on to their belief in themselves, others, and options in the future.

Positive Affirmations

In addition to listening and containing the fears and feelings expressed by your partner after trauma, it is also important to recognize and celebrate your partner's positive events and accomplishments, no matter how big or small. One study found that partners' recognition and affirmation of positive experiences and events in each other's lives play an important part in strengthening their relationship (Gable, Gonzaga, and Strachman 2006).

After traumatic events, particularly those that involve the death of a comrade, a dear friend, or a loved one, there is a tendency to feel that celebration of one's own life events is disloyal and inappropriate and shows a lack of reverence. We invite you to consider the thinking of Lt. Col. Dave Grossman (2004, 354), who reminds those in the military, "When someone gives his life to save your life ... Your moral, sacred responsibility is to lead the fullest, richest, best life you can." Celebration of life and each other gives you the strength to recover as well as to hold on to the memories of those you have loved. Even if it is now months after the original trauma, positively affirming each other's successes and good experiences builds resiliency both now and in the future.

Exercise: Affirming the Positive

Over the course of a week, make note of your partner's positive achievements, big or small (such as a great meal he cooked, her new job, the room she painted, the degree he earned). Affirm the positives as much as you notice the negatives.

Connection and Social Support

As we stated earlier, the most important component in recovery is a meaningful and supportive connection, and your relationship with your partner may be the most valuable connection in the recovery process. Research on the relationship between psychological buffers, hopelessness, and suicidal thoughts found that perceived social support was more important in reducing thoughts of suicide than improved life or improved self-esteem (Chioqueta and Stiles 2007).

Support Networks

When evaluating and building your couple resiliency, take some time to discuss how you are using your outside support networks. To do this, ask yourself the following questions:

- How do we preserve privacy for ourselves as a couple while receiving help from other sources of support, such as family members, neighbors, friends, and coworkers?

- Do our friends help us strengthen our relationship and further our recovery?

- How do we avoid the well-meaning judgments by outsiders about either of us or our relationship?

- How do new friends and associates fit into our life as a couple?

- Are we able to recognize, evaluate, and openly discuss issues of envy, jealousy, and possessiveness in our relationship?

- Are we each able to recognize when outside friendships are interfering with the exclusivity and confidentiality of our relationship?

- Are we aware that if we keep an outside relationship secret—no matter how supportive it may feel—it compromises the intimacy and resiliency between us as partners?

Recognition of, Respect for, and Reinforcement of Each Other's Resiliency Traits

Each of us possesses enduring positive qualities or traits that characterize us as an individual and are reflected in the fabric of our life's journey. These might include physical strength, intelligence, interpersonal skills, independence, sense of humor, creativity, and spirituality. These resiliency traits are often the foundation of or rationale for a person's coping skills, those strategies and behaviors that assist in times of stress. They are what we utilize to take the edge off, calm ourselves down, or sustain ourselves during a lengthy ordeal. Sometimes they come into play almost imperceptibly during the ups and downs of every day; at other times we may use them more consciously—when we are aware that we are going through a particularly difficult time. Similarly, over time couples develop resiliency traits that characterize their relationship and help get them through the rough times together. Couple resiliency is formed by a combination of the individual traits of each partner and the traits that emerge from the "we" they have created.

In the aftermath of trauma, it is common for one or both partners to feel so unlike themselves that they have difficulty finding those traits, even those they have always relied upon. One way of enhancing your couple resiliency is to help one another remember and utilize your individual resiliency traits. Being reminded of them can be tremendously reassuring and helpful at a time when you feel disconnected from the self you once were. For example, reminding him, when he feels vulnerable and defeated by an injury, that his problem solving has always been a major contribution to your lives regardless of whether he is sitting or standing, or complimenting her on her ability to refocus after the hurricane and turn wherever you have lived into a home, recognizes individual resiliency and fosters your recovery as a couple.

Exercise: Recognizing Resiliency Traits

Take a moment now and think about the resiliency traits you share as a couple. Ask yourselves, "What have we used to cope with this crisis or other crises in the past?" Looking at the traits that have helped you during stressful times will remind you that you have strengths as a couple. You may begin to realize, for example, that no matter what happens, you can both depend on her social skills, his memory, or your collective ability to laugh together, turn to your faith, or connect with family for additional support. Remembering what you bring together to the relationship is itself a resiliency trait.

Laughter and Sense of Humor

Certainly, one partner may have a stronger sense of humor than the other, but the ability of a couple to laugh together is extremely reparative and restorative in the aftermath of life's unexpected events. Maybe it comes through in your banter with other people in a hospital waiting room, the memory of the motel room you rented after the fire, or the e-mails sent home from Iraq. Regardless of how it's expressed, laughter has been called the shortest distance between two people. In relationships, humor has been reported to promote intimacy, belonging, and cohesiveness (Ziv 1988). Humor can be a resiliency strategy in and of itself. Spontaneously laughing and finding a way to make your partner laugh, especially when things are tense, is an important aspect of connection and soothing. It changes you physically, it enhances breathing, it is aerobic, and it is intimate (Godfrey 2004; Martin 2002). In short, it makes something good happen between you and your partner.

Handling Similarities and Differences

The power in any couple comes from the partners' belief in the "we"—the recognition that in certain ways the couple is greater than the sum of its parts. Believing in their "we" comes from recognizing and utilizing similarities and differences, balancing dependency and autonomy, and being able to agree and disagree in strong and safe ways.

Exercise: Self-Reflection and Recognition

Separately answer the following questions and then compare your answers.

* Is one of you street smart while the other is book smart? Is each of you strong in both areas?

* Are you different in how you express thoughts, feelings, anger, or pain?

* Is there a balance *within* each of you in your ability to be dependent and independent? Is there a similar balance *between* both of you? Does she depend on you to know more about what the children need? Do you depend upon her to know more about the finances?

* Can each of you be assertive about your needs or concerns as well as receptive to the other's needs or concerns?

* Is one of you the more assertive and the other the more receptive, and does that work?

Exercise: Couple Effectiveness List

Write down five ways in which you and your partner are most alike and five ways in which you are most different. Comparing both lists, make a list of the similarities that have worked for you as a couple. How have these similarities factored into your post-trauma recovery up to this point? Next, take a look at the differences on your lists. Where have differences balanced one another out, and where have they created strain? Have you been able to talk about this or work it through some other way? What differences have been most helpful to both of you? Discussing this together, add to your combined list the differences that have been beneficial in handling the traumatic event(s) you have faced. The list you have just created is your couple effectiveness list—your cheat sheet that shows how your differences and similarities join together to create your strength as a couple.

The Couple as a Team

Your mutually held belief that you function effectively as a team and can handle life's challenges together is a key factor in your strength as a couple. So far, we have helped you to think about your individual resiliency traits and the importance of recognizing and acknowledging them together. However, this does not necessarily equal effective teamwork. As is the case in sports, the fact that individual players have talent and skill does not automatically ensure their effectiveness as a team. A couple's ability to work as a team is based on mutual trust and includes communication skills, problem-solving skills, seeing things from different vantage points, managing disagreements and anger, forgiveness, and the capacity for hope.

Communication Skills

A couple's communication skills include the following:

* Being able to listen to your partner's opinion

* Giving and getting information and feedback

* Respecting your different perceptions

* Clarifying each other's ideas

* Being able to come to some verbal agreement, even if the decision is to think about it and talk again later

This is not easy to do, especially when one or both of you feel strongly about the issue. You will find it helpful, therefore, to have a problem-solving framework that reinforces positive communication and supports communication skills.

Problem-Solving Skills

Whether we are considering a sports team, a corporate team, or a couple, an essential ingredient for effective functioning is the capacity to problem solve (Levi 2007; Norman 2000). Being able to problem solve implies trust, an ability to collaborate, and a wish for a resolution that is mutually beneficial. Because differences and complementary skills make for creative and very often superior solutions, a couple's capacity to problem solve almost always adds to their sense of mastery and resiliency. In our workshops helping couples reconnect after trauma, we directly observed the benefit that couples derived from practicing couples problem-solving skills. In order to problem solve as a couple in a collaborative way, consider the following steps:

1. **Assess the problem.** Do you both understand it? What are the causes? How does it affect each of you?

2. **Brainstorm all possible responses.** Discuss possible actions you have tried—individually or tried as a couple—to solve this. Brainstorm and write down any or all other action you might try.

3. **Evaluate the pros and cons of each of the actions.** Do you need more information to really make a decisions? Do you need to try out a partial solution before you make a final plan? Should you agree to postpone or to think more individually about the problem and then come back with new ideas or possible solutions?

4. **Identify which of you is best able to handle the actions you are considering.** Should you each handle a certain aspect of the response?

5. **Decide upon a strategy or plan of action.** Don't be afraid to try out a temporary plan or solution.

6. **Evaluate the results.** Use curiosity and willingness—rather than blame—to gather information for further problem solving, if needed.

7. **Future planning.** Consider whether new, revised, or different plans are needed in the future.

Remember: Do not be afraid to compromise. Be motivated by the benefits to both of you—and to your relationship—when you choose your solution.

Exercise: Problem-Solving Communication

Select an issue that is currently of concern—something that one or both of you feel needs discussion and eventual resolution. Use the problem-solving steps listed previously to talk about the issue. Afterward, evaluate your discussion. Did you use the communication skills we described? Were you able to listen to your partner's opinion without interrupting or getting upset? Were you able to both give and ask for information and feedback? How did you show respect for your partner when he or she was expressing different perceptions or ideas? Was your partner able to experience this? Can you restate your partner's position on the issue? Can you let him or her know what you feel is resolved at this point and what needs further discussion? Can you agree on a plan to come back to the topic?

As you evaluate yourself and give each other feedback regarding your answers, try to be open to learning more about the communication skills that you know are valuable and that you want to improve.

Ability to See and Experience from Different Vantage Points

Your ability to see yourself and your partner from a different perspective is an important aspect of being an effective team. The factors involved in this skill are as follows:

- **Empathy.** To put yourself in the shoes of your partner and try to see and feel things from that vantage point.

- **Feeling understood.** To feel that your partner is empathetic toward you and can experience things from your point of view.

- **Observing your impact on your partner.** How do you affect him?

- **Considering your partner's impact on you.** How does he affect you?

Strategy: From Observation to Improvement

As a result of your observation from different vantage points, do a self-evaluation to determine those areas of self-improvement that would enhance the resiliency of you as a couple. Ask yourself, "Can I show empathy? Do I make my partner feel understood? Can I observe and understand my impact on my partner? Can I allow my partner to know his or her impact on me?"

For example, if you realize that as you are discussing a problem you keep cutting off your partner, you might work on waiting until he or she is finished, taking notes, or making a plan so that each has a set amount of time to speak. If you keep avoiding discussing a problem because you are afraid the discussion will cause a fight, you might begin by mentioning this fear and perhaps practice using the problem-solving guidelines listed previously. Or, if you realize, for example, that you discuss most problems with your family or friends before you ever ask your partner's opinion, and your partner feels marginalized or discounted, you might discuss this together and agree to first share your thoughts with each other before seeking the help of family or friends.

Remember, if your partner is owning or sharing something he or she does that disrupts your success as a couple, be receptive and supportive—your partner is risking change for both your sakes.

Managing Disagreements and Anger

The ability to handle disagreements and anger is crucial for maintaining and promoting couple resiliency, because it ensures that you will be able to withstand the inevitable disagreements that couples have.

As we discussed in chapter 3, it's beneficial to use anger management techniques, which can become valuable couple resiliency traits. An anger management plan, for example, provides a couple with strategies for defusing an argument, fair fighting, and conflict resolution (see chapter 3).

Forgiveness

An important couple resiliency trait related to managing disagreements and anger is forgiveness. Forgiveness implies the recognition that one has been hurt by another, and the willingness to release the negative thoughts and feelings toward the offending partner. Forgiveness is not the same as condoning negative behavior or complying out of dependency or fear—it is about the wish to go on, to let go of anger, retaliation, or revenge.

Forgiveness is often made possible by the apology of the other partner, usually acknowledging that an offense has occurred and admitting fault. An apology shows that the partner who has offended feels bad about the offense and cares about the other who is hurt. Accordingly, apologies usually acknowledge what has happened, convey remorse, and sometimes express a wish for reparation. In couples, an apology helps to restore safety, dignity, and power.

For example, if your partner tells you at the last minute that he is not going with you to your friend's wedding, which has been planned for months, you may feel both enraged and embarrassed. The flower and note of apology he gives you that evening may not take away the awkwardness you felt while attending the wedding alone. However, you might feel more inclined to forgive him and move on if he lets you know his reasons and that he is sorry. Perhaps he writes in his note that he just didn't want to face people but should have gone for your sake—if so, you'll be much more likely to let it go.

Apologies and forgiveness can differ in degree and behavior. Sometimes a partner's act of unloading the dishwasher is enough of an apology for the other to understand, forgive, and go on. Sometimes the offense is great and the pain inflicted warrants a verbal apology, a healing discussion, and the promise of doing things better next time. For example, if she has once again used household money to make a purchase without your knowledge, putting you both in more debt, then you have much more to discuss and she may need to do much more to foster recovery and forgiveness. However, apologies and forgiveness cannot be demanded—they are spontaneous responses to the belief that neither of you is perfect but together you can recover and grow as people and partners.

The Capacity for Hope

In her consideration of resilience and hope, trauma expert Yael Danieli (1994) tells us that hope is the ability to have options. When people look into the future and see only the traumatic past, they face a hopeless picture. They have no options; they cannot plan or wish or dream about the future. According to her, the greatest source of hope is the feeling of belonging. Belonging, be it to a military squad, a church, a community, a cause, or a partner, can instill the belief in possible options, even if circumstances are painful or difficult. Throughout history, the thought of another person or group has kept people alive. In a sense it is this power of belonging that makes the connection between a couple such a source of resiliency and hope. With her next to you, you can succeed despite the war injury; with him by your side, you can fight the illness. Together you can rebuild, heal, and have hope for the future.

Common Couple Values and Goals

Common or shared values both reflect and foster resiliency in couples. Couples may share intellectual pursuits, humanitarian interests, involvement in music or art, or spirituality. In fact, spirituality, whether in the form of affiliation with organized religions or personalized belief in a higher power, has been shown to foster resiliency in the face of and aftermath of trauma and disaster (McIntosh, Silver, and Wortman 1993). Given that trauma outstrips one's ability to fathom what has occurred, and limits a person's capacity to trust the goodness or justice in the world, people often seek solace and answers in some form of spirituality that transcends the ordinary physical limits of time, space, matter, and energy. Not surprisingly, spirituality is a powerful source of strength for couples when it's shared by partners (Vaughn, Call, and Heaton 1997).

Mutual Long-Term Goals

A sign of a couple's bond is their ability to have mutual long-term goals. Essentially, such goals usually reflect a couple's commitment—they expect to stay together. When a couple is able to begin making mutual long-term goals after trauma, they are stepping beyond the trauma with hope and a belief in the future. Whether they are planning a new house, a move across the country, another baby, a new business, a plan to get more training, or a decision to change locations to deal with a handicap or disability, their ability to plan together both reflects and enhances their resiliency.

Sometimes one aspect of a couple's long-term plan involves a mission that is directly associated with the trauma they have faced. Perhaps they plan to help other parents who have lost children, raise money for the cure of a certain illness, or personally lend a hand to other local veterans and their families; these kinds of humanitarian volunteer efforts offer them a way to make positive meaning of their experiences.

Post-traumatic Growth

While most of the literature related to trauma and its aftermath focuses on the difficulties that individuals and couples encounter, increasing attention is being given not only to resiliency factors but also to the concept of post-traumatic growth (Tedeschi, Park, and Calhoun 1998). Experts have chosen this term specifically because it acknowledges that after trauma some individuals surpass their previous levels of functioning as evidenced by their improved psychological functioning and a shift in their adaptation and awareness of the importance and value of life. The types of growth that people report are primarily in three areas. First, they notice changes in self-perception, including increased self-reliance and reduced vulnerability. Next, they see changes in interpersonal relationships, especially increased self-disclosure, emotional expression, and compassion—they're more likely to be honest and forthcoming with friends about their thoughts and feelings and feel more connected to others. Finally, they experience changes in their philosophy of life— perhaps they reestablish their priorities, so they "don't sweat the small stuff" and find new appreciation and meaning in life. Each of these areas is important, but the area of interpersonal growth can have the greatest impact on your relationship.

Have You Grown?

Perhaps in the process of working on your recovery from trauma, including your use of some of the exercises and strategies in this book, you have recognized that you are more in touch with your feelings and more comfortable with compassion, self-disclosure, and emotional expression. Of course, neither of you would have chosen this path to achieve a greater emotional connection, but your growth and its effect on your relationship are great benefits that will improve your life together for a long time to come.

Exercise: Reflection on Post-traumatic Growth

Take a moment to consider the way you have come to think about and deal with the traumatic event(s) you have experienced. Where have you put this trauma in the context of your life story as a couple? How has this position changed with time, information, and acceptance? Are you now looking at not just what you have lost but also what you have gained? How has your outlook on life changed? Are you more optimistic than you were? Can you work together to move beyond the fear of the next bad thing to a perspective that allows you to say, "We have survived this—we can survive anything"? A positive, hopeful outlook is integral to resiliency. Recognize the change in yourself and your relationship, and know that you have grown.

Exercise: If You Can Dream It, You Can Do It, Together

Write a letter to your partner as if you were writing five years from now. Look back on what you have been through and how your relationship has weathered the storm. Reflect on what you remember and what you value in your partner and in the relationship. Think about how you and the relationship have changed in the last five years. What have you come to enjoy and treasure?

Now, back in the present, ask yourself what dreams of yours can become realities.

Summary

Traumatic events assault our bonds with others and the sense of being connected to someone else. They rupture us in a way that makes us move away from ourselves and the people we love. We hope you see that your relationship need not be the collateral damage of trauma, but rather an invaluable resource. As a couple, you have been healing together, facing pain, and drawing upon your resiliency to recover your feeling of being whole, good, and connected. It is our hope that you will continue to heal together in a way that makes the impossible *possible*.

Recommended Reading

Armstrong, K., S. Best, and P. Domenici. 2006. *Courage after Fire: Coping Strategies for Troops Returning from Iraq and Afghanistan and Their Families.* Berkeley, CA: Ulysses Press.

Cantrell, B., and C. Dean. 2005. *Down Range: To Iraq and Back.* Seattle: Wordsmith Publishing.

Ferguson, D. 2006. *Reptiles in Love: Ending Destructive Fights and Evolving Toward More Loving Relationships.* San Francisco: Jossey-Bass.

Fisher, H. 2004. *Why We Love: The Nature and Chemistry of Romantic Love.* New York: Henry Holt and Company.

Grossman, D., and L. Christensen. 2004. *On Combat: The Psychology and Physiology of Deadly Conflict in War and Peace.* N.p.: PPCT Research Publications.

Henry, V. E. 2004. *Death Work: Police, Trauma, and the Psychology of Survival.* New York: Oxford University Press.

Herman, J. 1997. *Trauma and Recovery.* New York: Basic Books.

Johnson, S. M. 2002. *Emotionally Focused Couple Therapy with Trauma Survivors: Strengthening Attachment Bonds.* New York: Guilford Press.

Levine, P. 1997. *Waking the Tiger: Healing Trauma.* Berkeley, CA: North Atlantic Books.

Mitchell, S. A. 2002. *Can Love Last? The Fate of Romance Over Time.* New York: W. W. Norton.

Reese, J. T., and C. Castellano. 2007. *Law Enforcement Families: The Ultimate Backup.* Williamsburg, VA: Richmond Hill Press.

Stone, V. 2002. *Cops Don't Cry: A Book of Help and Hope for Police Families.* Ontario, Canada: Creative Bound.

Wachtel, E. F. 2000. *We Love Each Other, but … Simple Secrets to Strengthen Your Relationship and Make Love Last.* New York: St. Martin's Griffin.

Walton, C. 1996. *When There Are No Words: Finding Your Way to Cope with Loss and Grief.* Ventura, CA: Pathfinder Publications.

Weiss, R., and J. Schneider. 2006. *Untangling the Web: Sex, Porn, and Fantasy Obsession in the Internet Age.* New York: Alyson Books.

References

American Heritage Dictionary. 1993. *American Heritage College Dictionary*. 3rd ed. New York: Houghton Mifflin Company.

American Psychiatric Association. 2000. *Diagnostic and Statistical Manual of Mental Disorders* (DSM-IV-TR). 4th ed. Washington, DC: American Psychiatric Association.

Arzi, N. B., Z. Solomon, and R. Dekel. 2000. Secondary traumatization among wives of PTSD and post-concussion casualties: Distress, caregiver burden and psychological separation. *Brain Injury* 14:725–36.

Baldwin, D. S. 2001. Depression and sexual dysfunction. *British Medical Bulletin* 57:81–99.

Basson, R. 2003. Biopsychosocial models of women's sexual response: Applications to management of "desire disorders." *Sexual and Relationship Therapy* 18 (1): 107–15.

Berkowitz, L. 1990. On the formation and regulation of anger and aggression: A cognitive-neoassociationistic analysis. *American Psychologist* 45 (4): 2494–2503.

Blechner, M. J. 1998. The analysis and creation of dream meaning: Interpersonal intrapsychic and neurobiological perspectives. *Contemporary Psychoanalysis* 25 (4): 639–54.

Bonanno, G. A. 2004. Loss, trauma, and human resilience: Have we underestimated the human capacity to thrive after extremely aversive events? *American Psychologist* 59 (1): 20–28.

Boulanger, G. 2002. Wounded by reality: The collapse of the self in adult onset trauma. *Contemporary Psychoanalysis* 38 (1): 45–77.

Chemtob, C. M., R. W. Novaco, R. S. Harnada, and D. M. Gross. 1997. Cognitive-behavioral treatment for severe anger in posttraumatic stress disorder. *Journal of Consulting and Clinical Psychology* 65 (1): 184–89.

Chioqueta, A. P., and T. C. Stiles. 2007. The relationship between psychological buffers, hopelessness and suicidal ideation: Identification of protective factors. *Crisis* 28 (2): 667–73.

Coalson, B. 1995. Nightmare help: Treatment of trauma survivors with PTSD. *Psychotherapy: Theory, Research, Practice, Training* 32 (3): 381–88.

Cupach, W. R., and J. Comstock. 1990. Satisfaction with sexual communication in marriage: Links to sexual satisfaction and dyadic adjustment. *Journal of Social and Personal Relationships* 7:179–86.

Danieli, Y. 1994. Resilience and hope. In *Children Worldwide,* edited by G. Lejeune. Geneva: International Catholic Bureau.

De Silva, P. 2001. Impact of trauma on sexual functioning and sexual relationships. *Sexual and Relationship Therapy* 16 (3): 269–78.

Feeny, N. C., L. A. Zoellner, and E. B. Foa. 2000. Anger, dissociation, and posttraumatic stress disorder among female assault victims. *Journal of Traumatic Stress* 13:459.

Feldman-Summers, S., P. E. Gordon, and J. R. Meagher. 1979. The impact of rape on sexual satisfaction. *Journal of Abnormal Psychology* 88 (1): 101–5.

Figley, C. R. 1983. Catastrophes: An overview of family reaction. In *Stress and the Family: Coping with Catastrophe, Vol. 2,* edited by C. R. Figley and H. I. McCubbin. New York: Brunner/Mazel.

———. 2005. Strangers at home: Comment on Dirkzwager, Bramsen, Ader, and van der Ploeg (2005). *Journal of Family Psychology* 19 (2): 1–7.

Fisher, H. 2004. *Why We Love: The Nature and Chemistry of Romantic Love.* New York: Henry Holt and Company.

Fossage, J. L. 1997. The organizing functions of dream mentation. *Contemporary Psychoanalysis* 33 (3): 429–58.

Gable, S. L., G. C. Gonzaga, and A. Strachman. 2006. Will you be there for me when things go right? Supportive responses to positive event disclosures. *Journal of Personality and Social Psychology* 91 (5): 904–17.

Galovski, T., and J. A. Lyons. 2003. Psychological sequelae of combat violence: A review of the impact of PTSD on the veteran's family and possible interventions. *Aggression and Violent Behavior* 9:477–501.

Garfield, P. 1995. *Creative Dreaming: Plan and Control Your Dreams to Develop Creativity, Overcome Fears, Solve Problems, and Create a Better Self.* New York: Fireside.

Godfrey, J. R. 2004. Toward optimal health: The experts discuss therapeutic humor. *Journal of Women's Health* 13 (5): 474–79.

Gordon, T. 1970. *Parent Effectiveness Training: The Tested New Way to Raise Responsible Children.* New York: David McKay Co.

Grossman, D., and L. Christensen. 2004. *On Combat: The Psychology and Physiology of Deadly Conflict in War and Peace.* N.p.: PPCT Research Publications.

Hatfield, E. 1988. Passionate and companionate love. In *The Psychology of Love*, edited by R. J. Sternberg and M. L. Barnes. New Haven, CT: Yale University Press.

Hatfield, E., S. Sprecher, J. Traupmann Pillemer, D. Greenberger, and P. Wexler. 1989. Gender differences in what is desired in the sexual relationship. *Journal of Psychology and Human Sexuality* 1 (2): 39–52.

Henry, V. E. 2004. *Death Work: Police, Trauma, and the Psychology of Survival.* New York: Oxford University Press.

Herman, J. 1997. *Trauma and Recovery.* New York: Basic Books.

Hobfoll, S. E. 1989. Conservation of resources: A new attempt at conceptualizing stress. *American Psychologist* 44:513–24.

Institute of Medicine. 2003. *Preparing for the Psychological Consequences of Terrorism.* Washington, DC: National Academies Press.

Janoff-Bulman, R. 1989. Assumptive worlds and the stress of traumatic events. *Social Cognition* 7:113–16.

Johnson, S. M. 2002. *Emotionally Focused Couple Therapy with Trauma Survivors: Strengthening Attachment Bonds.* New York: Guilford Press.

Kazantzakis, N. 2003. In *The Book of Comfort: The Perfect Daily Companion* by H. K. Suh. New York: Black Dog & Leventhal Publishers.

Kulka, R. A., W. E. Schlenger, J. A. Fairbank, R. L. Hough, B. K. Jordan, C. R. Marmar, and D. S. Weiss. 1990. *Trauma and the Vietnam War Generation.* New York: Brunner/Mazel.

Lane, C., and S. E. Hobfoll. 1992. How loss affects anger and alienates potential supporters. *Journal of Consulting and Clinical Psychology* 60 (6): 935–42.

Lansky, M. 2000. Shame dynamics in the psychotherapy of the patient with PTSD: A viewpoint. *Journal of the American Academy of Psychoanalysis* 28:133–46.

Lehky, S. R. 2000. Fine discrimination of faces can be performed rapidly. *Journal of Cognitive Neuroscience* 12:848–55.

Levi, D. 2007. *Group Dynamics for Teams.* 2d ed. Los Angeles: Sage Publications.

Levin, R., and T. A. Nielsen. 2007. Disturbed dreaming, posttraumatic stress disorder, and affect distress: A review and neurocognitive model. *Psychological Bulletin* 133 (3): 482–528.

Levine, P. 1997. *Waking the Tiger: Healing Trauma.* Berkeley, CA: North Atlantic Books.

Levitin, D. J. 2006. *This Is Your Brain on Music: The Science of a Human Obsession.* New York: Penguin.

Lindy, J. D. 1986. The trauma membrane and other clinical concepts derived from psychotherapeutic work with survivors of natural disasters. *Psychiatric Annals* 15 (3; March): 153–60.

Maddi, S. R. 2002. The story of hardiness: Twenty years of theorizing, research, and practice. *Consulting Psychology Journal: Practice and Research* 54 (3): 175–85.

Martin, R. A. 2002. Is laughter the best medicine? Humor, laughter and physical health. *Current Directions in Psychological Science* 11 (6): 216–20.

Matsakis, A. 1996. *Vietnam Wives: Facing the Challenges of Life with Veterans Suffering Post-traumatic Stress.* Baltimore: Sidran Press.

McFarlane, A. C., and G. Girolamo. 1996. The nature of traumatic stressors and the epidemiology of posttraumatic reactions. In *Traumatic Stress: The Effects of Overwhelming Experience on Mind, Body and Society,* edited by B. A. van der Kolk, A. C. McFarlane, and L. Weisaeth. New York: Guilford Press.

McFarlane, A. C., and R. Yehuda. 1996. Resilience, vulnerability, and the course of posttraumatic reactions. In *Traumatic Stress: The Effects of Overwhelming Experience on Mind, Body and Society,* edited by B. A. van der Kolk, A. C. McFarlane, and L. Weisaeth. New York: Guilford Press.

McIntosh, D., R. Silver, and C. Wortman. 1993. Religion's role in adjustment to a negative life event: Coping with the loss of a child. *Journal of Personality and Social Psychology* 65 (4): 812–21.

McPherson-Sexton, S. A. 2006. Normal memory versus traumatic memory formation: Does traumatic stress damage the brain? *Journal of Police Crisis Negotiations* 6 (2): 65–78.

Mezey, G., and M. King. 1989. The effects of sexual assault on men: A survey of twenty-two victims. *Psychological Medicine* 19: 205–99.

Mills, B., and G. Turnbull. 2004. Broken hearts and mending bodies: The impact of trauma on intimacy. *Sexual and Relationship Therapy* 19 (3): 265–89.

Mitchell, S. A. 2002. *Can Love Last? The Fate of Romance Over Time.* New York: W. W. Norton.

Norman, E. 2000. *Resiliency Enhancement: Putting the Strengths Perspective into Social Work.* New York: Columbia University Press.

Ong, A. D., C. S. Bergeman, T. L. Bisconti, and K. A. Wallace. 2006. Psychological resilience, positive emotions, and successful adaptation to stress in later life. *Journal of Personality and Social Psychology* 91 (4): 730–49.

Ørner, R. 2004. A new evidence base for making early intervention in emergency services complementary to officers' preferred adjustment and coping strategies. In *Reconstructing Early Intervention After Trauma: Innovations in the Care of Survivors,* edited by R. Ørner and U. Schnyder. Oxford, UK: Oxford University Press.

Orth, U., and E. Wieland. 2006. Anger, hostility, and posttraumatic stress disorder in trauma-exposed adults: A meta-analysis. *Journal of Consulting and Clinical Psychology* 74 (4): 698–706.

Pennebaker, J. W., K. K. Kiecolt-Glaser, and R. Glaser. 1988. Disclosure of traumas and immune function: Health implications for psychotherapy. *Journal of Consulting and Clinical Psychology* 56:239–45.

Perel, E. 2003. Erotic intelligence. *Psychotherapy Networker* May/June.

Phillips, A. 2006. *Side Effects*. New York: Harper Perennial.

Rogers, C. 1989. *The Carl Rogers Reader*. New York: Houghton Mifflin.

Roisman, G. J. 2005. Conceptual clarifications in the study of resilience. *American Psychologist* 60:264–65.

Rudofossi, D. 2007. *Working with Traumatized Police Officer–Patients: A Clinician's Guide to Complex PTSD Syndromes in Public Safety Professionals*. Amityville, NY: Baywood Publishing.

Ruscio, A. M., F. W. Weathers, L. A. King, and D. W. King. 2002. Male war-zone veterans' perceived relationships with their children: The importance of emotional numbing. *Journal of Traumatic Stress* 15 (5): 351–57.

Scanzoni, L. D., and J. Scanzoni. 1988. *Men, Women and Change: A Sociology of Marriage and Family*. New York: McGraw-Hill.

Schore, A. N. 2003. *Affect Regulation and the Repair of the Self*. New York: W. W. Norton.

Schumacher, J. A., and K. E. Leonard. 2005. Husbands' and wives' marital adjustment, verbal aggression, and physical aggression as longitudinal predictors of physical aggression in early marriage. *Journal of Consulting and Clinical Psychology* 73 (1): 28–37.

Shalev, A. Y. 1992. Posttraumatic stress disorder among injured survivors of a terrorist attack: Predictive value of early intrusion and avoidance symptoms. *Journal of Nervous and Mental Disease* 180:505–9.

———. 2005. Treating survivors in the acute aftermath of traumatic events. The International Society for Traumatic Stress Studies, http://www.istss.org/terrorism/Treating%20Survivors%20of%20 Traumatic%20Events.pdf (accessed September 14, 2007).

Shem, S., and J. Surrey. 1998 *We Have to Talk: Healing Dialogues Between Women and Men*. New York: Basic Books.

Solomon, Z. 1993. *Combat Stress Reactions: The Enduring Toll of War*. New York: Plenum.

Taft, C. T., A. P. Pless, L. J. Stalans, K. C. Koenen, L. A. King, and D. W. King. 2005. Risk factors for partner violence among a national sample of combat veterans. *Journal of Consulting and Clinical Psychology* 73:151–59.

Taft, C. T., D. S. Vogt, A. D. Marshall, J. Panuzio, and B. L. Niles. 2007. Aggression among combat veterans: Relationships with combat exposure and symptoms of posttraumatic stress disorder, dysphoria, and anxiety. *Journal of Traumatic Stress* 20 (2): 135–45.

Tedeschi, R. G., and R. P. Kilmer. 2005. Assessing strengths, resilience, and growth to guide clinical interventions. *Professional Psychology: Research and Practice* 36 (3): 230–37.

Tedeschi, R. G., C. L. Park, and L. G. Calhoun. 1998. *Posttraumatic Growth: Positive Changes in the Aftermath of Crisis*. Mahwahm, NJ: Lawrence, Erlbaum Associates.

Ursano, R. J., T. A. Grieger, and J. E. McCarroll. 1996. Prevention of posttraumatic stress: Consultation, training, and early treatment. In *Traumatic Stress: The Effects of Overwhelming Experience on Mind, Body and Society,* edited by B. A. van der Kolk, A. C. McFarlane, and L. Weisaeth. New York: Guilford Press.

van der Kolk, B. A. 1996a. The body keeps the score: Approaches to the psychobiology of posttraumatic stress disorder. In *Traumatic Stress: The Effects of Overwhelming Experience on Mind, Body and Society,* edited by B. A. van der Kolk, A. C. McFarlane, and L. Weisaeth. New York: Guilford Press.

————. 1996b. Trauma and memory. In *Traumatic Stress: The Effects of Overwhelming Experience on Mind, Body and Society,* edited by B. A. van der Kolk, A. C. McFarlane, and L. Weisaeth. New York: Guilford Press.

van der Kolk, B. A., and R. Fisler. 1995. Dissociation and the fragmentary nature of traumatic memories: Review and experimental confirmation. *Journal of Traumatic Stress* 8 (4): 505–25.

van der Kolk, B. A., C. Perry, and J. Herman. 1991. Childhood origins of self-destructive behavior. *American Journal of Psychiatry* 148:1665–71.

van der Kolk, B. A., and A. C. McFarlane. 1996. The black hole of trauma. In *Traumatic Stress: The Effects of Overwhelming Experience on Mind, Body and Society,* edited by B. A. van der Kolk, A. C. McFarlane, and L. Weisaeth. New York: Guilford Press.

van der Kolk, B. A., A. C. McFarlane, and O. van der Hart. 1996. A general approach to treatment of posttraumatic stress disorder. In *Traumatic Stress: The Effects of Overwhelming Experience on Mind, Body and Society,* edited by B. A. van der Kolk, A. C. McFarlane, and L. Weisaeth. New York: Guilford Press.

van der Kolk, B. A., A. C. McFarlane, and L. Weisaeth, eds. 1996. *Traumatic Stress: The Effects of Overwhelming Experience on Mind, Body and Society.* New York: Guilford Press.

Van Vliet, K. J. 2008. Shame and resilience in adulthood: A grounded theory study. *Journal of Counseling Psychology* 55 (2): 233–45.

Vaughn, R., A. Call, and T. B. Heaton. 1997. Religious influence on marital stability. *Journal for the Scientific Study of Religion* 36 (3; September): 382–92.

Walker, J., J. Archer, and M. Davies. 2005. Effects of rape on men: A descriptive analysis. *Archives of Sexual Behavior* 34 (1): 69–80.

Weiss, R., and J. Schneider. 2006. *Untangling the Web: Sex, Porn, and Fantasy Obsession in the Internet Age.* New York: Alyson Books.

Wilkes, G. 2002. Introduction: A second generation of resilience research. *Journal of Clinical Psychology* 58:229–32.

Wilson, J. P. 1990. Conflict, stress and growth: The effects of war on psychosocial development among Vietnam veterans. In *Strangers at Home: Vietnam Veterans Since the War,* edited by C. R. Figley and S. Leventman. New York: Brunner/Mazul.

Ziv, A. 1988. Humor's role in married life. *Humor: International Journal of Humor Research* 1:223–29.

Notes

Notes

Notes

Notes

Notes

Suzanne B. Phillips, Psy.D., ABPP, is a psychologist who has worked with couples and with trauma for more than twenty-five years. She is adjunct professor in the clinical doctoral program of Long Island University and is on the faculty of the postdoctoral programs of the Derner Institute of Adelphi University, NY, and the Suffolk Institute for Psychotherapy and Psychoanalysis, NY. She has published in the trauma field, trained professionals, and provided direct service to help civilians and uniformed responders cope with trauma. She and Dianne Kane created *Couples Connection*, a program used to help more than 400 firefighter couples recover after 9/11. She is coeditor of *Public Mental Health Service Delivery Protocols: Group Interventions for Disaster Preparedness and Response*. She is also in private practice in Northport, NY.

Dianne Kane, DSW, CGP, is a clinical social worker who has been involved in the development and delivery of employee assistance and trauma intervention services to uniformed personnel in the New York City area since 1994. She is currently assistant director of the counseling unit serving the Fire Department of New York City and, in that capacity, has been instrumental in the post-9/11 recovery effort for a workforce of more than 13,000 personnel. She and Suzanne Phillips worked with more than 400 FDNY couples assisting in their recovery from trauma. Kane has been on the faculty of Hunter College School of Social Work since 1988. She is coauthor of *FDNY Crisis Counseling: Innovative Response to Firefighters, Families, and Communities.*